To Make a Duck Happy

TO MAKE A

DUCK HAPPY

by Carol E. Lester

Illustrations by Feodor Rojankovsky

HARPER & ROW, PUBLISHERS
New York, Evanston, and London

FIRST EDITION

LIBRARY OF CONGRESS CATALOG CARD NUMBER: 73-83605

This book is lovingly dedicated to little ducks everywhere, hoping it will help people understand them a bit better.

Contents

Preface

MY FATHER SHOULD have been a naturalist, for he was that at heart. His great interest in plants, insects, snakes, birds, and animals was shared by my mother and conveyed to his three children.

Naturally my sister, brother, and I had a succession of much-loved pets. In England, where we lived until I was five, we had white mice, a white Spitz, a box turtle, and a hedgehog. In this country, our first pet was a long-suffering cat named Wussie. Two families of rabbits, guinea pigs, two tiny wild rabbits needing a foster home, a canary, and two baby red squirrels also needing a home, followed. We were taught that responsibility to a furred or feathered friend cannot be waived at whim; they must be loved and cared for in sickness and health. It was a valuable lesson.

After a petless gap, my son had a dachshund and later a boxer for a while; then the duckling Patsy was given to me, followed later by Peter. These two have been more fun than any of the other pets. Each has his own distinctly individual temperament, each his own likes and dislikes, and from them

I have learned how like people are birds in their affections, tempers, jealousies, and tastes.

The lives and experiences of these two Pekin ducks, as well as those of their mallard and other friends, have been so interesting I wanted to share them with others, both for pleasure and greater understanding.

CHAPTER 1

Duckling . . . Becomes Duck

"PEEEEP! PEEEEEP!"

The small yellow duckling scrambled out of the box in which she had arrived and immediately ran to me, uttering shrill cries. She scuttered about my feet, following every step I took. In her infant desperation to belong to someone, she had adopted me. I had suddenly become Mother to a feathered child!

Patsy came into our lives unexpectedly. One day at work I said to a friend that I'd like to have a pet duck. It seemed appropriate, as my son and I were then living in an ark on the Sausalito waterfront. Shortly afterward, my friend's small nephew went to a fair and won a baby duckling at a raffle. Soon the boy's family had to move, and my friend brought the duckling to me—unannounced. It was a delightful surprise!

I was entranced to have this downy little person with her tiny webbed feet and minute beak for a pet. As a child I had, each Easter, bought one of the little stuffed ducklings the dime stores used to sell—fortunately no longer—and cherished it all year. Now I had a live one.

I picked her up and cuddled her in my hands to examine her. Thick yellow down covered the small body. Her wings were little stumps, featherless as yet, but showing signs of sprouting. Only her tail had the beginnings of real feathers, and those barely showed as tiny stiff quills. Both her beak and feet were a light yellow. I loved her immediately and hoped she wouldn't grow out of her enchanting baby stage too fast.

When I put her down on the floor and walked into the kitchen she followed me, and I offered her water. This she savored beakful by beakful, tilting her head back each time to let it trickle down her throat. Then she ate a little lettuce and tomato, and a few bits of bread. Not knowing she was coming, I had no mash or chick feed to give her.

That first day Patsy was very excited about her new surroundings. Like most ducklings, she had probably been raised in that impersonal, unresponsive device, the incubator, her longing for a warm feathered mother met only with a light bulb. During the short interval with the little boy, I knew she had been kept in a carton in a garage—a lonely existence. No wonder she was thrilled to have found a loving, attentive mother and to be allowed the run of a house. She followed me everywhere, eagerly exploring all the rooms but not straying from my feet for a moment.

When I prepared dinner that evening, Patsy pattered near as I walked from refrigerator to stove to table, so that I had to be constantly alert not to step on her. Once or twice, however, the large human foot did bear down on a delicate small toe and there was an unhappy "Peeeeep!" If I walked faster than she could follow and rounded a doorway so that for an instant I was lost to sight, there were shrill cries of alarm.

The traumatic moment came when I went into the bathroom faster than her little legs could keep up with me, and shut the door. There was a stunned silence. I heard her run into the bedroom, the dining room, the living room, and back to the kitchen, her tiny cries growing to thin, piercing screams. The moment I opened the door and she saw me, she gave her first soft peeps of satisfaction.

That night at bedtime, I filled a small carton with sweet hay and put her in it by the side of my bed. I didn't want her to feel lonely ever again. She pulled the hay this way and that with her tiny beak, arranging it to her liking, then crouched down, keeping her bright little eyes, black-seeming amidst the yellow down, upon me. Before I put out the light, she rose up at intervals to peer over the side of the box to be sure I was still there. Even after the room was dark she occasionally gave an anxious, inquiring "Peeeep?" to which I answered reassuringly, "Peeeep-peeeeeep." Soon the small noises ceased and she slept.

I had come to Sausalito some years before, following a long visit home, having decided I would rather live in northern California than in Long Beach, where I'd been during the war. Having a great affinity for water, I was thrilled to live again close to such a large body of it as San Francisco Bay, with the Pacific Ocean only three miles away over the hills to the west. Evening after evening I walked along the waterfront, delighting in the expansive view of dark water and city lights about the Bay . . . a scintillating, colorful example of the art of pointillism.

At intervals along the waterfront I discovered, scattered in among the yachts, shipbuilding sheds, and the great schooner *Pacific Queen*, little groups of arks perched above the water on pilings. One of these groups I noticed particularly as it was set off by itself in a pondlike area. Whenever I walked past I thought how remote, how almost forlorn, these arks looked; weatherbeaten, pilings askew—especially the one nearest the Bay—and especially on a rainy day when sky, water, and arks were all only different shades of a dismal gray. Little did I think I should ever live there in one, and that when I did, I should love it!

When my son and I first came to Sausalito, we lived for several years in part of a very old house until the owner decided to pull it down and build apartments. We had to find a new home. I looked and looked with no success. Then, just two days before the old house was to be razed, a real estate woman phoned to say she had found a place for us. It was the ark I had particularly noticed.

When we went with the agent to look at it, we crossed the water by means of an uncertain plank walk, supported by hollow pilings, which led from the shore past one group of arks to the ark nearest the Bay, which was neatly painted white, with green trim. Although it looked comfortable inside, I demurred a little at its rather makeshift appearance and the weatherbeaten look of the surroundings. Aptly, the woman replied, "You can live in a house any day, but how often do you have a chance to live in an ark?" It was a good point— we moved in. And truly, ark life proved unique.

The small backwater of the Bay where the arks were I came to call the Pond. It had been formed when as part of a projected "development" the clamshell and mud bottom of the Bay had been dredged and dumped to form a short roadway which jutted out at right angles to Sausalito's waterfront street. The road then curved around to the north to become a wide bar about two hundred feet long, separating the Pond from the Bay. Fortunately for us and our neighbors, the plans progressed no further. Projecting northward, the bar narrowed to form a fingerlike low mud spit. The water between it and the mainland formed a lagoon, bounded on the north by a long pier jutting out into the Bay.

Straddled over the Pond here and there on pilings were six individual arks, and a conglomerate group of ancient ones set side by side, built forty years before for Greek fishermen. (An ark is a dwelling built on a floating barge bottom. When the bottom deteriorates, very often the ark is set up on pilings near the shore, reached from land by a plank walk. Our ark, however, had originally been built on pilings.) Three of the separate arks faced the street and were reached by decking in front of them. The other three, including ours, were reached by the plank walk that crossed the Pond from the shore near the street to the mud bar. Our ark had decks both front and back, and on the side between us and our neighbor; it was entered through a door off the walkway, the only door. Flower boxes of bush sedums and geraniums brightened the deck in front, while at the back stood a long box I filled with a variety of flowers.

Although put together of bits and pieces, our new home was very livable. It was forty feet long and eighteen feet wide. The living room occupied all of the far end and from its windows we had wide views eastward to the golden hills of Tiburon and darkly wooded Belvedere, two miles across the Bay. Northward one looked past the long pier with its shipbuilding sheds toward Mount Tamalpais, the highest point in Marin County, whose spurs stretched forth in many directions, adding hill and forest charm to the area. The south side faced an ark about ten feet away. Behind the living room were the dining room and a large walk-in closet, and behind those, the kitchen, bedroom, and bath.

The ark floors sagged a bit due to sinking piles, and our

beds had a constant list to port, but who needs an even keel for sleeping? Ceilings were low, and my son and any tall friends had to stoop going through the doorways. I loved the sun and air around our little home, and such oddities as being able to look down the sink drain to the water to see a coot's red eye peering up from below, and the convenience of a "Disposall" in the form of tides and birds.

As the days went by, we learned the vagaries of local tides. At low low tide the Pond was almost emptied, and at high high tide wind-driven waves sometimes slapped the joists and one could almost imagine oneself afloat. It was a very appropriate home for a small duck!

Patsy's first few days were ones of discovery. Because she was so small I was afraid she might fall through the deck fencing into the water, so to keep her safe from this and from possibly ill-natured dogs, I made her a large cage which stood on the deck behind the ark, beneath the bedroom window.

From it she could peer down to the water below and watch the coots as they swam beneath the arks, croaking and looking for food. Since it was summer when Patsy arrived, there were no ducks, but occasionally she could see an egret or heron wading near the shore. Near our ark were several tall poles on which sea gulls loved to perch. With lordly stance they waited, keen eyes surveying the Pond, ready to swoop down and snatch at anything edible, even that already claimed by the coots. Sometimes two gulls tussled over a floating morsel, crying with rage as they did so. Eagerly Patsy followed this drama of bird life.

Also out on the deck was a zinc tub into which I put her each day for a swim. Round and round she would go, bobbing about and paddling happily for long periods, then call me to help her out when she'd had enough.

After being outside awhile, Patsy would become lonely and quack to come in, so I would bring her into the ark. There she always stayed close by me, her bright eyes watching everything I did.

In about four weeks, Patsy was big enough not to need the cage. She was no longer a child but a fascinating adolescent. First her tail feathers had developed, then her wings sprouted rows of quills. Gradually the yellow down on her body had given way to soft white feathers all over. Finally her quills were fully grown and she could flap full-feathered wings. The tiny duckling had become a charming small duck.

Patsy always loved the kitchen, the source of food. As long as I was working there, she kept me company. If I was peeling potatoes, she'd reach for each piece as it fell from the peeler and gobble it down. Bits of celery, carrot, or lettuce were more than acceptable, and liver a treat. If I forgot to offer her a piece of whatever was being prepared for us, she would delicately nibble at my feet, the way ducks attract each other's attention. Her favorite food was peas.

I taught her to jump for a pea. I'd hold one above her while her eyes focused expectantly upon it, and say, "Jump, Patsy!" She'd give a spring with her flat feet about two inches off the floor and open her beak to catch the tasty morsel as it fell. Sometimes she missed it, and I sensed the chagrin she felt at her clumsiness. A word of encouragement was needed—assurance that she was really a very clever little duck. Then she'd hastily search about for the lost pea. When seen, it was quickly run after—one couldn't let even a single such delicacy disappear.

If Patsy was inside the ark, she joined us at mealtimes. She liked to stand by the corner of the table between my son and me, keeping a sharp eye on both of us in case we should let something drop for her. If nothing appeared, she'd twitch at our napkins impatiently or tug at our clothes to remind us of her presence, and the forthcoming manna was gobbled up with gusto. Her appeals to taste what we were eating were so charming we couldn't often resist. She liked being with people and taking part in their activities.

When Patsy was three or four months old, I asked the vet whether a duck could be housebroken, but he told me ducks could not be trained. Just like human babies, baby ducks "go" often, and at first I had constantly to pick up after her. As Patsy grew, there were longer and longer intervals between "goes." She became very conscious of her droppings since I always came immediately with toilet paper to whisk them away. She began to call me ahead of time on occasions; as soon as I came she'd "go," watching closely while I did the janitor bit. Sometimes she'd call me afterward in a loud voice, "Ma, come quick—I did something!" and then observe how the matter was dealt with.

About once a day a duck (a collective noun meaning either male or female) does a really potent number. One day I said, "Ooooh, Patsy!" in a tone of horror as I rushed the offending result outdoors and into the watery "wastebasket." She immediately stretched out her neck and flattened her little body upon the floor, saying in a most apologetic, tremulous tone, "Peeeeeep-peeeeeeeeeep." It was obvious she felt dreadfully humiliated and was asking my pardon for being so obnoxious. Quickly I said, "That's all right, Patsy. You can't help it," and petted her to assure her she was still loved. Up she got and with flapping wings ran about for a moment, quacking in evident relief. In future I tried to remember not to express my feelings at such times, but if I did forget she always went through the same cringing motions, asking my forgiveness.

Several cats lived near us, two with an artist neighbor. They were all very curious about the little duckling at first and often climbed the deck fence to sit and watch her doings. I found they were not above stealing her liver bits and learned to give those to her indoors at night for her supper.

There was also a dog in the same household, a very friendly boxer named Corny who did her best to play with Patsy. Although the dog was much bigger, Patsy had no fear of her at all. In characteristic boxer way, Corny would walk up close and switch her rear end toward Patsy. With a dog, it would have been a gentle push meaning "Let's play!" But Patsy was too small to push, so Corny would crouch down on her front paws and bark, trying to entice Patsy to bounce around with her. Sometimes she'd smell her. That always brought an indignant quack and the "go-away" sign ducks make by lowering their beaks to the ground, advancing menacingly toward the unwanted one.

One day I introduced Patsy to an epicurean delight—snails. The walkway led from our ark past the one where the cats and boxer lived, to solid ground near the street where the "snail bushes" grew. These were fleshy-leaved succulents which snails doted on—to their undoing. Especially after a shower.

I'd say, "Come on, Patsy, let's go and look for snails," and she'd hotfoot it after me, all agog at the tasty prospect. Sometimes there were so many she could find them herself with her sharp eyes and she would make quick jabs at the clinging snails. Other times they were scarce, and I had to search the middle of the large bushes where she couldn't reach. If it was a good snail day, she'd waddle back to the ark with crop loaded and faintly jangling. She was always very quiet after these trips, I noticed, a little overcome it seemed by so much rich food.

Some days a sudden longing for snails would come upon her and she'd wander out of the house and down the walkway to the bushes by herself. Usually it was safe but strange dogs did come by, not as friendly as Corny, so I didn't like her to go alone. I taught her to wait at the top of the two steps outside the ark door until she had permission. She'd walk to the edge of the top step and quack to me, in the ark, meaning, "May I go down to the snail bushes?" If I said "Okay, Patsy" she'd half jump down the steps, and off she'd go; however, I soon followed to keep an eye on her.

Once she found a huge slug near the snail bushes. It was her first and she had no idea what she was up against. She tried to mangle the poor thing to get it down, but it was very slimy and much too large for a duckling, so she finally spat it out. Her beak was full of goo which almost choked her. I had to pick a bunch of grass and wipe it out. After that she regarded slugs with interest but did no more sampling until much later, when she learned that baby slugs are delicate enough for a lady duck to enjoy.

Worms were another special delight. Patsy was very happy whenever I got the spade to dig them for her. She'd stand right in the hole with her big feet thoroughly in the way, afraid of missing any. Her quick eyes saw them before I did; the small protruding end was immediately seized and the worm pulled forth. Somehow she never broke them in two as I often did. If I got tired of digging she'd urge me on by pecking my feet, or scold me for not producing any. She could certainly play the tyrant if she chose. She seemed to crave fresh meat, so I tried to please her by producing it whenever possible during the short springtime, when the ground was soft and damp and worms lived near the surface.

Patsy continued to sleep by my bed for several months. She always wanted to settle down before I did and, if I was too long about it, would start a plaintive peeping, ceasing only when the light was out.

After that, she often liked to have a little conversation which began with an inquiring "Peeeep?" If I didn't answer, she asked again. When I replied "Peeep" she'd continue with a sentence, "Peeeep-peeeep-peeeeeep-peeeep?" in a rising note. I'd answer, "Peeeeep-peeeeeeep," and she would continue. If I tired of peeping to her and there was silence after her last remarks, she'd ask again with an insistent note, "Peeeep-peeeeep-peeeep?" over and over until I said something. Evidently it wasn't polite for me to end the conversation until she was ready.

Sometimes during the night she'd wake and make a few remarks, but always in a very soft voice—an instinct, perhaps, to be quiet at night and not let an enemy know one's whereabouts.

Patsy was an early riser and at dawn's first light would wake me with her tiny soft voice. Set free onto the floor, she would patter to the kitchen and eat the breakfast I had put out the night before. Then, satisfied, she would return to stand patiently by my bed.

If the sleeper slept too long, there would be a gentle question: "Peeep-peeeep-peeeeeeep?" Aren't you *ever* going to get up? I'd look down to see a yellow beak pressed against the side of the bed and two beady eyes fixed upon me. One could not long resist such an appeal and I'd rise to take her outside to the deck to begin another happy day of experience and adventure.

CHAPTER 2

The Pond

PATSY SEEMED VERY content with her little world at the Pond. Life in the ark was full of interesting experiences, she found, and out on the deck she never tired of watching the other birds. Her territory was further enlarged by the bar, which was somewhat hummocky and covered down to the water's edge with yellow-flowered genista and broom brushes, coarse grasses, poppies, lupins, and other wildflowers. Here she scrambled up and down over the hillocks, searching through the grass tufts for bugs and poking in the soft damp places for worms, whenever I allowed her over there.

Extending out into the Pond from the northern end of the bar, at the entrance to the lagoon, was a small peninsula, humped in the middle, which Patsy liked to visit also. Only a little vegetation grew on the hump since during high tide most of this peninsula was submerged, but around the mud edges flourished a succulent dark-green weed which many of the water birds enjoyed. Patsy too sampled it and found it tasty. From the peninsula she could get a closer view of the lagoon and the mud spit which on wintry, windy days was often covered with sea gulls seeking shelter from the fury of ocean storms.

Our ark neighbors were interesting too. Near the street and alongside the walk was an old fishing boat, laid up on the shore many years before as unseaworthy although not uninhabitable. A succession of footloose souls occupied it. Each of the various occupants fixed up some deficient part—mending the leaking roof, attending to the ancient plumbing, or stretching burlap on the cabin walls. Some hung art objects to liven the interior. One painted a few flowerpots and filled them with geraniums, making a brave splash of color about the entrance.

Next to the boat and parallel with the walkway was another white ark with green trim. Its front deck faced the Bay and was gaily decorated with pots of flowers, climbing vines, and even a small tree. Here lived the artist-owner of the cats and Corny.

What matter if the deck door no longer hung in place? A curtain served as well, both as visual and thermal barrier. And if a few holes in the kitchen floor revealed the water underneath, one soon learned to step adroitly and avoid them. The patio deck, furnished with such rugged items as a cable-reel table, made a fine outdoor workshop as well as a carefree spot for resting and entertaining. What yacht owner could ask for more than was at hand here? Sun, blue skies, an expansive view, and the interesting life on the waterfront and Bay.

Our ark, I was delighted to find, provided a splendid ringside seat for watching marine and bird activities both nearby and farther away on the Bay. Sailboats of all sizes, motorboats, tugs, and ocean-going dredges passed back and forth, while lone pelicans, migrating ducks, and long lines of cormorants flew the airways. From the kitchen and living-room windows I could constantly watch the daily lives of the many water and land birds who came to the Pond and lagoon. It was a fascinating scene.

Each day the tides surging through the Golden Gate, some three miles away, swept up the Bay into the lagoon, and slowly filled the Pond from its lowest ebb of inches to over six feet in the deepest part. Each high tide brought a new pondful of water, flotsam and jetsam, small water creatures, and fish.

The Pond was a haven for water birds. Sea gulls, coots, egrets, grebes, blue and white herons, sandpipers, rails, and several varieties of duck gathered at various times, not to mention the land birds—crows, Brewer's blackbirds, warblers, a kingfisher, sparrows, and visiting tits—which frequented the Pond. There were exciting goings-on for a small duck to watch, and naturally she soon wanted to join the swimmers.

Patsy's first swim almost ended in a drowning!

Because I didn't know how far she might go once in that fine expanse of water, I had fortunately taken the precaution of making her a collar of soft toweling, with a cord attached. With this on, she pattered down the bank into the water and, delighted with this new experience, swam rapidly away, small feet flipping back and forth.

When she was some twenty feet from the bank, I noticed her body was getting lower and lower in the water—she was sinking! Hurriedly, I started to pull her in. Because her feathers were so waterlogged, her head was barely above the surface. When I pulled on the cord, her head went under. So it was a matter of pulling her fast while her head was submerged, giving her a short breather for air, and then pulling again. At last she was safely on the bank! She could scarcely stagger for the load of water. Many wing-flaps and body-shakes were needed to throw it off, so the rest could be preened away. As a small duck, Patsy apparently did not have enough oil in the gland above her tail to keep her feathers waterproof. This is the oil gland which ducks pinch while preening themselves, distributing the oil along their feathers at the same time. In a few weeks the gland functioned normally, and she floated buoyantly.

From this fearsome experience Patsy learned caution and for some time never swam far from the shore or stayed in long. Never again did she need to wear her collar.

That first year another terrifying thing happened. Due to her ignorant human mother, poor Patsy suffered convulsions—not once, but twice!

One day out on the deck she suddenly began to stagger about and almost fell over. Alarmed, I picked her up, rushed indoors, and phoned the vet. He thought it must be convulsions and told me to bring her over immediately, adding that perhaps she had picked up some fowl disease which a vitamin-B shot would clear up. But, as I didn't know the real cause, it happened again several days later, a more severe attack. This time I held her upright for several minutes—and prayed hard. In a few moments it was all over. Later, reading a government bulletin on ducks, I learned that sour mash can cause convulsions. I had sometimes left half-eaten bowls of mash for Patsy to finish, and having no duck mother to warn her, she had eaten it. Well, we all learn. She never touched old mash again.

All birds have a variety of feathers, most marvelous in their structure. With ducks, there is of course an undercoating of soft down. In addition, many body feathers have down on the part closest to the body; this blends into true feathering at the tip. Straight narrow feathers cover the head, with tiny, minute ones growing around the outer eyelids, giving protection and forming eyelashes. Sleek curved feathers pad out the breast. On the wings, strong quills of varying sizes are arranged in three rows, and on the body large curved feathers, very soft, cover and warm the upheld foot when snoozing. The pointed tail is formed by stiff straight feathers which can be spread fanwise to make a useful comb for straightening the head feathers. Next to his tail, a drake has one or two curly feathers proudly proclaiming his sex.

Although this feather padding on a duck may be an inch or so in depth, the slightest touch upon an outside feather is

felt immediately, just as we feel a touch upon our skin. Any disarrangement is uncomfortable and must be straightened at once with wing flaps, a body-shake or vigorous preening. Good grooming keeps a duck busy!

From the beginning, Patsy was always particular about her appearance. She bathed frequently, afterward carefully preening each feather neatly into place. After a bath there was a thorough and systematic grooming. Between times the toilette was more casual—a light setting-to-rights of the breast feathers, a quick pinch of the oil gland above the tail, and vigorous head-smoothing by running her head upside down across her back, with a dab here and there, and a reaching-around to that area below the tail. The most difficult part was just between her legs. It meant either standing up very straight, neck stretched downward to its fullest so she could rake the area with her beak, or bending way around sideways—quite a strain on the neck muscles.

As she grew, I noticed Patsy's beak becoming a greenish color near its base while the hard tip turned black instead of yellow. This, I was told, was her mallard ancestry coming through. For although Patsy was a Pekin duck, originally these birds were bred from mallards in the country near the Chinese capital.

When Patsy was several months old, I learned of a woman who had house-trained her duck, so I tried to teach Patsy since she was so conscious about "going." I kept a paper on the floor for her but she failed to use it. After she'd "gone" on the linoleum, I'd put her on the paper saying, "Go ON the paper, Patsy, ON the paper," and show her that's where I put the wiped-up remains. She'd cock her head and eye it, but the idea didn't seem to register. Whenever she called beforehand, I'd rush to place a paper under her—and wait. Nothing doing.

As soon as I released her she'd step OFF the paper—and "go." Intelligent as she was in many ways, there seemed to be a mental block about this.

Although I kept trying, without success, Patsy did learn something else. When I put the paper near the bed and she flapped her wings, the breeze she created usually scooted it under the bed, and I would have to retrieve it. She watched this procedure several times. Then she noticed that if she was in the center of the room and flapped, the paper stayed put. After that, when Patsy was by the bed and wanted to exercise her wings, she walked to the center of the room, flapped hard, and walked back again. Deductive reasoning, I believe they call it—but of course only people are capable of that.

During Patsy's first spring at the ark, I was going away for a weekend, and having no one with whom to leave her, took her over to the vet, who had a small boarding home for dogs and cats where he lived. She was put into a large airy cage all to herself. I supplied plenty of foods she liked best for her three-day stay. The young attendant seemed very interested in her, and assured me he'd see that she had fresh water at all times and would be fed as I asked. I'm sure this was done.

But when I went to fetch her, she was standing forlornly, looking out of the cage. I picked her up, petted her, and put her into a carton in the car. She was very quiet, I noticed, and for the next two or three days didn't seem like herself. Then in two weeks' time she suddenly began to moult.

I phoned the vet to ask why, as it certainly wasn't the season. He told me that birds sometimes moult from shock, and that evidently Patsy's stay at his place had been sufficiently traumatic to bring it on.

When I thought a bit about it, I wasn't really surprised. To be removed from familiar surroundings where she enjoyed complete freedom to come and go, to be confined in a cage where she was surrounded by barking dogs and mewing cats (always distressing to her), to be fed by a stranger, with no knowledge she'd ever see home again—all this was naturally a great shock to her.

Later that summer I wanted to go to the mountains for a couple of weeks. It wasn't possible to take Patsy and since my son was away I couldn't leave her at home. I wondered where to find a temporary home for her. One day when I was walking along a pier in the yacht harbor, I saw two ducks swimming near a houseboat.

Hmmmmmm, I thought. I walked across the plank and knocked on the door.

The young girl who opened it was very friendly. She told me she and her husband had had the two Muscovy ducks for some time and let them swim in the Bay freely. When the ducks wanted to come out, they walked up a ramp to a deck on which their food was placed.

I explained my need of a home for Patsy during the two weeks I'd be gone and immediately the girl offered to take care of her. It seemed like a happy solution. However, I asked if I could bring Patsy over for a day and a night first, to see how she liked the living arrangements there.

When she met the Muscovies, they evidently struck her as rather strange birds. A Muscovy is white like a Pekin, but longer, with rough red skin over its forehead and face, trimmed with caruncles. Patsy had never seen one before.

The living area seemed to please her. She made for the ramp immediately and was soon in the water paddling about. In a short time she made friends with the other ducks. Her overnight visit was a great success. When my vacation began,

I left Patsy with the Muscovies, content that she would be happy and feel at home. On my return she was glad to see me and I could tell she had enjoyed her vacation too. This time I knew there would be no moulting later.

As she grew, Patsy developed several lovable little habits. She still preferred to be in the house with me part of the time. If I lay on the bed, reading, she'd stand close by, head tucked under wing, taking a pleasant nap.

She soon learned that a ringing phone must be answered. When I hurried toward it, her feet would fly as she too ran to the telephone. If I wasn't in sight when it rang, she would run to the table and stand directly under the phone, calling loudly for me to come. If I ran in from outdoors to answer it, a great emergency, she felt, she would follow and rush about the house, wings outspread, squawking.

Whenever she came into the house, she visited the kitchen first. Waddling through the living room and dining room, she always veered to the right just inside the kitchen doorway for a look at a certain spot where at one time I had put down her food; then on to the paper with her food and water bowls. After eating, she checked the garbage can to see if any tasty bits she might like had been carelessly thrown in.

Patsy was really quicker at understanding my language than I hers, and responded alertly to several words:

"Come here"—if accompanied by gestures, although she didn't always choose to comply!

"All gone"—when she hung around expectantly and poked in her bowl for more.

"No"—she learned this more quickly than a child, but you could see the struggle sometimes between doing what she wanted and pleasing her "mother."

"Spank"—oh, the ignominy of being caught by the neck and chastised lightly with a paper—feelings were hurt far, far more than feathers!

"Outside"—this meant she had to leave the ark and return to the deck. At this word she often ran to stand under the dining table, hoping I wouldn't see her.

"Bath," "pool," "pretty," and her favorites "peas" and "tomatoes," all assumed meaning for her.

When she wanted something Patsy could be most demanding. At first she began with quacks, then louder ones, and if no results were produced she let out a great big loud-mouthed "ARRRRRK! ARRRRRRRRRRK! ARRRRRRRRRRRRRRRRK!" This was "loud talking" which, if not curbed after a warning from me, was sure to be followed by "spanking."

"Do you want to be spanked for loud talking, Patsy?" I'd ask, a bit annoyed with her. An indignant voice would reply, "Kuk-kuk-kuk-kuk," not knuckling under one bit. But she knew I meant it, and it was sometimes pitiful to see this small being, possessed of quite a temper, trying hard to smother her feelings and going about grumbling to herself, bursting forth now and then with what she obviously felt was righteous indignation at her treatment. I tried hard to understand the causes of her various grievances and to rectify the justifiable ones, but we had trouble with semantics. It was really my fault, for I, like other people, have forgotten what we all used to know—and birds and animals still do—how to communicate by telepathy. Patsy must have thought me very stupid! No wonder she was annoyed.

CHAPTER 3

Laying That Egg

WHEN YOU WANT an egg, it's easy, isn't it? You just go to the refrigerator and get one, neatly ovoid like its brothers, out of the box. But did you ever consider the *laying* of that egg? It's WORK!

I always thought egg-laying was quite simple. All a hen had to do was twiddle around in a nest a bit, make a little effort, and there it was, white and shiny.

Not so. For one thing, she has to get up very early. While you are lolling in your bed, wrapped in sleep, some little feathered creature has already risen, prodded by nature to her almost-daily task. Around her, others may dream—the rooster, old hens, and young chicks. But she, poor soul, must cast sleep from her eyes (no steaming coffee cup for her), rise from her perch, and head for the nest to lay you that egg.

Yes, it's work.

Patsy began to lay eggs when just a few months old. I was always surprised at the number of adults who, ignorant of the production of eggs, inquired, "How can she lay eggs without a drake?" I explained that female birds are hatched with a certain quota of potential eggs within them. They can be laid as infertile eggs—or fertile. Patsy commenced, of course, with the former. She was still sleeping in the box by my bed, and one morning, very early, I awoke to a great commotion. I could hear her turning round and round. Scratch, scratch, SCRATCH! What in the world was going on?

I got out of bed, turned on the light, and looked in the box. Where previously there had been just a small hollow in the hay for sleeping, little Madame had now made herself a fine nest with her turnings and twiddlings, and was huddled down in it.

As she crouched, she scratched purposefully, first with one foot, then the other, over and over. Head down, tail up, she half circled the nest and scratched again. I gazed in wonder at this performance. I concluded that the effort of scratching must help propel the egg outward. More scratches alternated with cluckings. Then she gave a heave and brought forth a small egg.

I was thrilled! Patsy's first egg! How considerate of Nature to make the initial one easy, I thought, examining it with much interest.

"Oh, Patsy! What a beautiful egg!" I exclaimed. "What a clever duck to lay such a fine one."

She stood looking down at it, then prodded it gently with her beak as though a bit surprised at her accomplishment, and perhaps a little proud. Contentedly she settled down on it, and I went back to bed. I glanced at the clock. It was just after three A.M.

The next night I was again awakened by the scratching sound. This time the clock showed three-thirty. Patsy was again circling and circling around in her nest. Scratch, SCRATCH! "Quack, QUACK!" Her tone this time was serious and determined. She turned and turned, and scratched again. There was an earnestness in this night's performance that had been lacking before. It was evident that this egg was giving some difficulty.

More turnings, her head down, tail up. "Cluck-cluck!" She sounded like an old hen. On and on it went.

Four o'clock and no egg yet. She was plainly weary. The scratching grew more desperate. Then, with a few pain-filled clucks and a mighty heave, the egg came forth. What a monster! Almost twice the size of a hen's egg. It was the largest she ever laid. Exhausted, we both fell back into bed with relief.

From then on this became an early-morning performance. I learned that there is a laying cycle. It begins about three-thirty A.M., getting gradually later each day, the cycle eventually ending with an eight-thirty laying. After this latest lay, Patsy skipped a day; then the cycle began again about three-thirty.

When Patsy laid her egg early, she would sit on it and go to sleep again. If she laid it later, she would sit for perhaps a few minutes to an hour on her nest, then leave.

People often asked me, "What do you do with the eggs?" This always struck me as a curious question. Are we so far removed from rural life that the general thought is that only chickens lay eggs to eat? For duck eggs are delicious. The white is not yellowish like a hen's egg, but a clear pure white. The yolk is always a rich orange and usually much larger in relation to the whole egg than is a hen's egg. The shell has a slightly greenish tinge.

Each day I took the egg from Patsy's nest, showed her I was doing so, and praised and thanked her for it. I was happy to receive this daily gift. Usually I let the egg "rest" in the refrigerator a day or so before using it, as a "hot" egg didn't appeal to me.

Patsy was a good layer. The first year she produced an egg almost every day; the next year fewer, but still almost three hundred. After the second year the number declined. When her husband Peter arrived, she began to lay fertile eggs and made a few attempts at sitting on the clutch I let accumulate. But twenty-eight days is a long stretch and Patsy lacked the patience for motherhood. I understand this is not unusual for the Pekin ladies. It seems they are not strongly maternal and hatching must often be left to an obliging and motherly hen, or that mechanical mother, the incubator.

A duck's nest is very important to her. It is always kept clean, never fouled. Patsy clucked with delight whenever I gave her a fresh lot of hay to add to her nest or to make a new one. She prodded and pulled the hay with her beak, circling round and round until it was shaped to her liking.

Soon after Patsy began to lay, I decided she was big enough to sleep outdoors. I found a sturdy wooden box, minus top, turned it on its side, and boarded up half the aperture so it would be cozy and private inside. This I covered with tar paper against the rain and put it up against the front of the ark, just outside the living-room windows. Since I slept on the other side of the wall, I could still hear all the going-to-bed sounds—and the egg laying—and we could continue to have our bedtime conversations. It was a cozy arrangement.

Also, to give her more space than just the deck area, I built a pen on the bar of land that divided the Pond from the Bay. A narrow bridge about eight feet long with slat sides connected the pen on land to our deck, and little Madame could come and go above the water at her pleasure. I often watched her rear view with amusement as she crossed the bridge. A stiff fan of tail quills surmounted a mass of soft feathers, each of which pointed upwards, giving the triangle below the fan an upswept effect, while her two sturdy orange feet splodged majestically along the boards, causing a fascinating swing-and-sway movement.

Patsy liked the land pen where she had earth underfoot. When it rained, she loved digging in the soft ground for

grubs. Grass grew tall around the fencing, and a large tomato plant screened one corner, offering many of the tomatoes she so loved.

In another corner of the pen I made a lath house with a latticed shingle roof so sunlight could filter through. Filled with hay, it made a luxurious nesting place. In good weather she laid her eggs there, rather than in the wooden box on deck. It was charming to see the white, would-be-mother duck sitting like a queen in her bower.

A round plastic pool with inflated sides occupied the corner of the pen nearest the water, and in this Patsy often bathed and swam, delighting in dipping her head down and flinging water over her back to clean her feathers and refresh herself.

From the pen she had a much better view of the Pond and the other birds than she did from the deck. On sunny days when the tide was in, the Pond was a cheerful sight. The coot family, who lived there almost all year, often bathed along the edge of the peninsula. Standing ankle-deep in the water, they vigorously threw it over their stout black bodies.

Several white egrets fished in the Pond, at times as many as fifteen. More often, however, only three came, and I thought of them as brothers, christening them Edward, Everett, and Ernie—the smallest. Standing tall on their stalklike black legs, their white crests and chest feathers ruffled by the wind, the three "brothers" waded cautiously in the shallows, each foot upheld in turn as they proceeded. With snaked necks and heads bent low, they peered through the water, their dagger-like beaks poised. Suddenly one of them would strike out, seize a befuddled little fish crossways in his beak and hold it up; then, with a quick toss, he would turn the fish head first and swallow it.

If fish were not to be seen, they would "skitch-skitch" in

the mud, first with one foot, then the other, trying to scare up a small perch or minnow resting on the bottom. I noticed Ernie was the most ardent fisherman of the three. Even on a dull day when fish were difficult to find, his impatient mud-search was often rewarded while his less diligent brothers found little.

Sometimes bevies of sparrows searched the nearby weeds and bushes for seeds and insects, or boldly perched on the rim of the grain dish for a free meal. Afterward, crops comfortably distended, they clung to the top of the pen fence in rows, teetering back and forth, chattering excitedly.

One morning I came out to find Patsy in her lath house looking rather forlorn. There was no egg in her nest. She had been laying quite steadily, so this came as a surprise to me, but I decided she'd just skipped that day. The next day, however, again no egg.

On the third morning the mystery was solved. As I crossed the plank to the land pen, the neighbor's small black cocker spaniel squeezed himself under the fence and rushed off toward his ark. In the pen was the evidence of his intrusion—a smashed egg.

We had an egg addict next door!

Patsy stood beside the egg quacking very unhappily. No wonder. It was one thing for her "mother" to take her egg each day, for she knew from my thanks and praise that she gave me pleasure. But for a stranger to thus violate her nest and rob her of her daily offering was indeed a shock. I went over, stroked her feathers, and offered my sympathy for her loss.

I then went next door, caught the thief, led him back to the scene of his crime, and firmly applied a folded newspaper to his rear, while Patsy watched with acute interest. He howled his regrets and dashed off when released. This chastisement, plus a few sharp pecks from Madame when she was outside the pen and he ventured too near, evidently convinced him it wasn't worth trying again. He had learned his lesson.

As Patsy grew older, she laid eggs mostly in the spring, and by the time she was seven produced only a few each year. Sometimes, even though she'd laid none for several months, I'd hear her in the early mornings going through the egg-laying routine with much clucking, fervid scratching, and pitiful crying sounds which were sad to hear, for half an hour or more. She plainly seemed to be mourning her failure to produce eggs. Each time the sounds were so genuine I'd think surely she must have laid one. Each time the nest was empty.

CHAPTER 4

Public Appearances

W HEN ONLY SIX months old, Patsy made the front page of the *Independent Journal*, the Marin County paper. It was the twenty-third of December and perhaps news was scarce, but there she was, standing on a table in front of a mirror, admiring her new jacket. It was this unducklike garment which evoked the story.

Early in Patsy's first winter she caught cold. At night she slept by my bed. During the day she was outdoors most of the time. The change from warm house to outside chilliness brought on the cold, so she had to be kept indoors until she was well again. I wondered what I could do to prevent another illness when she returned to her regular routine.

Well, what do people do when they go outdoors? I asked myself. They wear a jacket to keep warm. I knew turkeys were very sensitive birds and often died of pneumonia in the winter cold unless they wore jackets. Why not get one for Patsy? It seemed a good idea.

I asked her vet if he knew where I might find such a jacket. He told me that turkeys wear poncholike leather garments with a head hole and two wing holes, which are put on them in the fall, to be worn day and night until spring. This didn't seem quite the thing, however, for a duck of such refined sensibilities as Madame.

Feeling rather foolish, I next inquired at pet shops. "Do you have a small dog jacket which might be suitable for a duck?" I asked. Some thought this an exceedingly odd question but tried to help when I explained the reason. There were jackets small enough, but I soon realized that dog coats make no provision for wings which need to be left free for flapping.

It seemed I would have to make one. After some thought about design and a few try-on sessions with my model, I finally evolved a smart little number made from part of a man's gray sweater, lined with Milium, and piped with red. Slipped over Patsy's head, the "jacket" completely covered her chest as far back as her legs. Two flaps went under her wings and were snapped together on top of her back so she could move her wings as she wished. When it was finished, I put it on her and stood her in front of a mirror so she could see herself. She stared and stared, and seemed to approve.

At first Patsy found it very strange to wear a garment and not be able to preen her feathers at all points. She'd try to pluck at them and find herself with a beakful of wool. She soon became fairly used to it, however, although she was never completely happy about the feel of wool under her wings, and kept twitching them at intervals. In the morning after she had her breakfast the routine was for her to don her jacket to be all set for outdoors.

She was very good about standing quietly while I put it on. First the hole went over her head; then I turned her around to face me, lifted her wings, and snapped the two ends together across her back. This procedure often unbalanced her and she

tilted forward so her beak hit the floor, but she accepted "getting dressed" without complaint. I often told her, "Oh, Patsy, you do look smart!" Like people in tight shoes, she seemed ready to suffer a little for such sincere approbation.

Soon after making the jacket, I was surprised when a reporter from the *Independent Journal* phoned to ask if he might interview Patsy. He had heard about her through the vet. It seemed that a duck wearing a coat was news.

When the reporter called at the ark, he asked all about Patsy's arrival, her living habits, and just why she wore the jacket. Later a photographer came to take her picture. I assumed the article would appear somewhere on the back pages, but the next day brought a surprise! There, right at the top of the front page, in two-column width, was Patsy's picture, with a long article beneath. Naturally, I showed Patsy her picture and read to her from the article.

Patsy's next honor was an oil painting of herself done by our neighbor artist and presented to me at Christmas. It was a charming likeness, capturing all her perkiness and independence. Sometimes I catch her taking a long look at it.

Patsy's greatest moment in the outside world was the day she attended a meeting in the Gold Room of the Sheraton-Palace Hotel in San Francisco.

The Gold Room is an ornate ballroom on the main floor. The occasion was a gathering of representatives of *Life* magazine, of which I was one at the time, to launch a sales special. Patsy had been invited to attend as a humorous introduction to the program. Very much a spur-of-the-moment idea, there was no time to make her anything special to wear. So she put on her red-piped gray jacket, and to each "shoulder" I attached a large red LIFE cut from the magazine cover.

We drove to Second Street, parked in the garage opposite

the hotel, and entered the lobby, Patsy in her box. Never one to miss what goes on, she raised her head and noted all the activity. A few human heads raised too. Outside the Gold Room, we waited near the door in a hidden corner, since our act was to be a surprise.

The idea was for her to walk up to the platform, be introduced, and retire. In a strange place I knew she would never go ahead of me, but *would* follow me, especially if I was carrying something to eat. I had therefore brought a small bottle of peas—her favorite food.

When the chairman's remarks sounded the cue, I put Madame out onto the floor. Such a tiny figure in the huge ballroom. I walked ahead of her up the side aisle past the rows of people, holding the bottle in my hand by my side. Patsy followed, avid for the tasty peas. She scuttled the long length of the room on her little yellow feet, was helped up the steps and lifted onto the speakers' table. What a proud moment for a little duck. So many eyes upon her!

"May I introduce our newest *Life* representative, Patsy Duck!" the chairman said. Patsy stood up straight, showed off her LIFE emblems, and was heartily applauded as she left the platform. Back in her box, I praised her fine performance and rewarded her with the peas.

Is there any other duck who can say she has performed in the Gold Room of the Sheraton-Palace Hotel? Patsy can!

CHAPTER 5

A Husband Is Found

PATSY HAD A BUSY life, watching birds, digging worms, gathering snails, swimming with the wild ducks, visiting in the ark, and just snoozing on one leg for long periods of time. But she began to feel this wasn't quite enough—

Watching the mallard couples as they swam about, she obviously felt something was missing from her life—a mate. Each duck Patsy observed on the Pond had a handsomely feathered drake by her side and, naturally enough, she wanted one too. She tried to demonstrate her need by doing her mating dance before me, bobbing her head up and down, quacking all the while, and getting very annoyed because I wasn't a drake.

When she was about two years old her pleadings grew more frequent and I decided something would have to be done. A drake must be found.

First I looked in the newspaper. There were several ads of ducks for sale, but not a drake among them. I followed up one ad for fertile duck eggs, hoping the advertiser might have some mature male birds, but no luck here either. I asked friends but no one could give me a lead. It seemed all of Marin County was devoid of Pekin gentlemen.

Finally I wrote to the young man who had given me Patsy, asking him to search around Santa Cruz, where he now lived. After a time he found a farmer willing to sell one of the ducks he kept in an enclosure on his farm. Later my friend told me how the ducks lived there. The earth was bare, hard, and dusty. There was no pool, no water in which the birds could swim. A rude, covered area served as the only shelter. And for food, there was a wooden box with dry mash, a pan of warm, muddy water, and some exhausted lettuce leaves scattered on the ground. A "fringe" existence indeed!

There were about thirty ducks in the flock. My friend looked them over carefully. Patsy would be particular, he knew. This one was too scrawny; that one had a funny walk. His attention was caught by a drake who was outstanding for his large blue eyes and fine build. The big eyes settled it. He would surely be a romantic charmer for the little lady duck in Sausalito so anxiously awaiting a mate.

The young drake was caught, dropped into a carton, and handed to my friend, who put him on the floor of the car.

Like many people, my friend, though kindly at heart, did

not stop to consider that a bird has feelings and fears just as people have. To a young drake, ignorant of any life but that within his small orbit on the duck farm, the three-hour trip shut up in a small dark space must have been a nightmare. He could see nothing. He could neither raise his head nor turn around. Nor could he flap his wings. He was offered no drink of water, so essential to ducks, for his parched tongue. Poor fellow! To fright was added discomfort.

When my friend arrived and put the carton down on the living room floor, I was all agog. Patsy hurried in from the deck and looked expectantly at the box. Cautiously I opened the lid.

I caught only an instant's look at the newly arrived husband-to-be. I saw his broad orange beak, bigger than Patsy's, and large blue eyes staring up in terror. In a sudden flash of movement up shot his long white neck. Then with a strong flap and a powerful jump, he leapt, landing on the linoleum-covered floor, skidding along its slippery surface. Alarmed, he peered about, spotted the open door, and fled toward it. With a desperate lurch, and aided by his wildly flapping wings, he propelled himself outside.

We all rushed for the door in time to see his white form reach the end of the walkway and suddenly topple into the water with a loud splash. In spite of no swimming lessons, he swam quickly across the Pond, reached the farther shore, and climbed onto the land.

Patsy stood dumfounded! She too had had only a momentary view of a handsome drake—the prospective husband for whom she longed—only to see him disappear in an instant.

My friend ran around the edge of the Pond and after a chase caught the drake. We put him into the cage Patsy had used when she was small, out on the deck next to her nest box. There he cowered in a corner.

Well, the bridegroom had arrived! Scarcely domesticated, it seemed, but probably time and Patsy could alter that. I decided to call him Peter.

I went into the ark, filled a pan with water and another with grain, and brought them out on deck. As I approached the cage, Peter hissed and puffed up his feathers, eyeing me with horror. I wondered why he was so frightened, and then remembered my friend had said the farmer sold ducks for eating. Probably Peter had seen his relatives seized, their heads twisted round and round, and their limp bodies carried away. Poor darling! No wonder he was terrified. For all he knew, I might do the same to him. Everything in his world had suddenly gone topsy-turvy. What dreadful thing might happen next?

I realized, too, what his first encounter with water must have meant, for it was the first time he'd ever had a chance to swim. To be in such a large body of it, so cool, so fresh, must have been a wonderful feeling. And what intense disappointment to be captured and once more deposited in a small space with wire all round.

Opening the top of the cage, I put down the water and grain, closed the top and left Peter and Patsy alone. From inside the ark, I watched through the window.

Patsy continued to stand a little distance from the cage, staring and staring, while Peter made spasmodic movements inside. She seemed puzzled at his behavior, for his obvious fear of people was unknown to her. After a while she apparently tired of his company, crossed the bridge to the pen, and slid into the pool for a leisurely swim.

It was definitely not love at first sight on her part, at least.

He was a drake, to be sure, but far different from the self-assured, well-mannered mallard drakes she knew.

Peter stayed in the cage three days. By then he acted less frightened and would not start away when I went near him. I felt it would be safe to let him out, for it was obvious from the way he followed Patsy with his eyes that he was exceedingly interested in this charming lady duck.

I lifted Peter out of the cage, set him on the deck, and sat down some distance away to watch. For a few moments he couldn't believe his good fortune. Out of that awful cage at last! Free—within the confines of the railing about the deck. He stretched himself tall, raised his wings, and flapped, and flapped again. How good it felt to exercise them. Then, scarcely waiting to settle his feathers, he lunged toward Patsy and grabbed her neck feathers!

Madame let out a shocked squawk. How dare he? What kind of boorish drake was this? None of the mallards approached their ladies in this crude manner. She had watched them often and she knew the procedure a gentlemanly drake should follow.

First he swam up beside the lady of his choice and quacked pleasantly to her. Small talk was exchanged, the duck chattering casually. They enjoyed a bath together, then dabbled along the shore looking for waterweed, or joined a group of ducks for a swim. And after some time, if the lady responded, the drake led her away from the others to a secluded area and there made his intentions known through the ritual of the mating dance. Facing her, he would begin to bob his head up and down in jerky movements. If the duck was interested, she did the same. If she was not, she might respond with a few bobs, then turn away, making it plain he was not her choice, or at least not at that moment. If she was enamored of the gentleman, the bobbing increased in tempo and they would mate.

All this Patsy had seen. No wonder she was surprised at Peter's behavior. She shook herself loose from his grip and rushed along the deck, Peter right behind her. Across the bridge she went, trying to get rid of him. It was no use. He followed closely, his beak tickling her tail. Now in the land pen, she hurried up the pool steps and into the water, trying to lose him. He too scrambled up the steps and splashed in beside her, and once again caught hold of her neck feathers, her wing, her tail.

"Quack-quack!" Her plea was desperate and I had to answer it. I went out to the pen and shooed Peter away, not difficult to do as he wanted to be as far from me as possible. But the minute I left, he was after Patsy again.

Hour after hour, Patsy had no peace. She couldn't take a step without being followed. If she lay down for a nap, Peter would go over and prod her here and there with his hard beak, trying to give her love dabs—but how lacking in gentility! Up she'd get and wander round the deck, looking for an escape; but there was nowhere to hide. Finally she stood under the window and in desperate tones called to me inside to rescue her. I brought her in to have a much-needed nap.

In the following days, Peter tailed Patsy constantly. I knew no way of stopping him except to pen him up.

Peter's arrival meant a great change in Patsy's small world. Everything had to be shared now—the eating dish, the pool, the deck, the worms, the sleeping box—a stressful time! For Peter it was equally difficult, an uprooting from the familiar, plus the sudden shock of an entirely new life.

Thinking about this, I realized why Peter followed Patsy all the time. He felt strange and lonely. She was his own kind, the only friend he had. To be with her made him feel secure, and he needed security badly. He wanted her in sight every minute.

There were some things Peter liked very much about his new life, however. The food was gourmet compared to what he'd been used to. Crisp lettuce, celery, juicy tomatoes (how he loved those), cracked corn, milo—all heretofore unknown treats. And worms—apparently the tastiest beakful he'd ever encountered!

Peter's eating manners were very good. He always let Patsy have first choice of food, and waited till she'd had her fill before he ate. She could make no complaints about this. Apparently he complied completely with duck etiquette.

But his pool manners were something else. Before Peter came, one of Patsy's greatest pleasures had been swimming in her pool. Now it had to be shared—not only shared but relinquished at times, for Peter monopolized it until he'd finished bathing. I could see it irked her. Previously, she'd been able to get in and out any time she chose. Now that country lummox pushed in ahead of her, thrashing the surface with his wings, spraying water in every direction. If she tried to get in too, he would poke her until she left. He wanted it all to himself. Patsy often looked dejected at this treatment, but in a way I understood Peter's behavior. It was a new adventure to him and he could never get enough of it. To be in water was his greatest joy. Hour after hour he'd sit in the pool, churning up the water and playing about while Patsy waited her turn. There was actually room for both, but only rarely did Peter allow her to join him.

After a few weeks, Peter was let out to swim in the Pond with the mallards. How he enjoyed it! He soon became pop-

ular, and perhaps the admiration of the mallards helped Patsy
change her views about him. For her attitude *did* change.

Peter had persisted in his wooing of Patsy from the first day
he was free, even though she repulsed him again and again.
But in time her attitude softened. She evidently found it
pleasant to have Peter's company and no duck could have asked
for greater devotion than his.

I noticed too that little by little Peter's attentions became
more "couth." Perhaps some of the drakes gave him a few
hints. At any rate he became more refined in his actions, his
pokings more subtle and elegant the way proper love dabs
should be. Patsy even seemed to enjoy them when they sat
quietly together. And then of course he *was* a most handsome
drake with fine, upstanding posture, broad chest, strong wings.
A catch for any duck.

One sunny October afternoon, Peter's persistent courtship
was rewarded. Patsy made up her mind!

She and Peter were out swimming with the wild ducks, but
this day Peter indulged in no aquatic antics with his friends.
He swam at Patsy's side in a sedate mood, and after a while
led her away from the group and near the shore. Once again
he began the mating dance and quacked to her, as he had so

often before. Up and down his head bobbed rhythmically. Patsy, facing him, joined in. But this time she did not withdraw and turn away as before. This time she responded wholeheartedly—and they mated.

It has been a long and happy marriage.

CHAPTER 6

The Mallard Breakfast Club

TO PATSY AND PETER, the activities of the birds about us were an endless source of interest. Peter in his youth had seen no water birds, and being one himself he naturally felt a great kinship. During his first days with us that August, only a single coot and a few visiting grebes and egrets represented the water fraternity. There were some sea gulls, but they are partly land birds. Even these few he studied intently as they freely swam in the great watery expanse whose joys he had experienced but once.

Early in September the scene changed. Newcomers arrived and former residents returned, for during the summer many of the Pond regulars went elsewhere. First to come was a large family of coots, noisily greeted by the lone one who had remained through the year. Seemingly coots are an unhappy lot. The ladies grumble and nag; the gentlemen scold and peck. And all the little coots copy their parents. Their croaking disagreements always filled the air.

I often threw edible bits overboard to help fill the empty crops of our neighbors—sea gulls, sandpipers, and others. The coots came to depend on this largesse as they are not fish eaters. They also kept a sharp eye on the flotsam that floated in on the tide and nibbled at the water plants. If one coot grasped something edible, another would lower his head and, with neck outstretched, pursue the finder. The latter would rush off, trying to gulp down the morsel before he was caught. If he wasn't quick enough there would be a tussle, with aggrieved complaints from the loser.

If a strange coot came to the Pond, one of the resident coot family would swim out to meet him, croaking disapproval and warnings. If the stranger did not retreat, the Pond coot would lower his head belligerently and threaten force. Usually the other coot, when made aware of his inadvertent invasion of family territory, swam hastily away, rising quickly and pattering across the water on his green feet until he felt safe.

But one coot was not to be intimidated by mere words.

While Patsy was bathing in her tub one day when still a duckling, we heard louder than usual cries from the coots below. I looked over the railing. Near the pilings was Mr. Coot, his family circling nearby. Approaching was a strange coot, a strong fine-looking male. He had much to say and his tone was arrogant.

As he came closer, Mr. Coot slowly swam to meet him, croaking in a low, threatening voice. The stranger paid no attention. It was apparent from his lordly bearing and loud demands he had no intention of leaving; he wished to usurp Mr. Coot's rights and take over the Pond. This Mr. Coot would not tolerate. The Pond was his territory.

An ultimatum was given by Mr. Coot: Retreat or fight.

The stranger continued his advance. When the birds were about a foot apart, suddenly each threw himself backward upon the water, lying upon it with wings outstretched, maintaining this posture by rotating his wings in arcs. They began to fight, each trying to rip the other's exposed and vulnerable abdomen with his feet. They clawed at each other viciously; sometimes one managed to whack the other with his wing.

Round and round they went in a circle, churning the water and throwing spray in all directions while their cries of anger mounted. Finally Mr. Coot delivered a decisive rip, for the other suddenly folded his wings and paddled away as fast as he could. Mr. Coot followed after hotly, his neck outthrust, causing the intruder to rise on his toes and with the aid of his wings patter swiftly across the water until he was safely out of the Pond.

The coot family, who had withdrawn to a safe distance while Mr. Coot defended the family rights, croaked their praises as the victor returned. I wondered if her husband's bravery would cause Mrs. Coot to treat him more graciously for a while. It did not!

The next to arrive in September were the small white egrets. Later that month the wild ducks arrived. We first saw them a few weeks after we moved to the ark. Early one mellow morning I looked out and was astonished to see the Pond occupied by about forty mallards sitting silently on the water. There had been no ducks before. When I opened the door to step out, several of the nearest shot up in alarm, and the others were tense and poised, ready to do likewise.

Later I learned that although the mallards had been coming to the Pond for several years they were always very wary and nervous at first, due to their hazardous trip south from the upper reaches of Canada, where they nested during the summer. Too often, people meant guns.

Intrigued by their numbers and shyness, I threw bits of bread into the shallow water near the bank. Not a duck stirred. I sensed they were very hungry, but even more fearful. Who could tell, from a duck's eye view, what might lurk behind the large tree-root on the bank, or the nearby bushes?

I stood absolutely still. Finally one small female swam toward the bank. Immediately a cautious drake headed her off. But she persisted, approaching closer and closer by fits and starts. At last she seized a piece of bread, gulped it down, and snatched hungrily at more.

Seeing this, some of the others gained a little confidence. Timorously they joined her in the shallows. Some of the older drakes still hung back, not yet ready to accept the seeming safety. Soon, however, all were avidly filling their empty crops.

I watched as they dipped up and down in the water after their meal, washing faces, preening feathers. For a few moments they rested, some swimming this way and that. Then one duck who had been moving among them in some agitation, apparently urging them to leave, rose swiftly from the water with a whir of wings and was followed by the others. Away they went in single file, heading south. At dusk they returned in little groups, and again spent the night and early morning at the Pond.

I bought some corn and the mallards soon came to expect the morning handout. Just after dawn an ever-increasing chorus of insistent quacks demanded their daily bread.

"Quack-quack! Quack-QUACK!" We want our grain! We want our grain! There was no use trying to sleep until they were appeased. The cries were too loud, too urgent.

If the tide was out at the usual feeding time, leaving only the muddy bottom, they waited silently in the lagoon an hour or so until the tide had crept into the Pond and filled the shallow areas where I threw the grain.

Other mornings when the tide ebbed early and they knew

the Pond would not fill soon, the mallards would waddle across the mud from the lagoon toward the ark, lurching up and down over the uneven bottom. They never seemed to look where they were going. Consequently their webbed feet fell into holes, throwing them off balance, causing them to trip over themselves. They disliked walking so far over the rough ground and there were a few small complaints as they stumbled along.

Mid-tide was the best time for feeding the ducks, for it created pools where they could wade in knee-deep water and gobble up the corn or milo I tossed them. Ducks love to slurp their food, and they delight in letting the water pour through their beaks while edible morsels are retained by the sawlike strainer along the edge of their upper beaks.

At high tide the steepness of the bank provided no small pools, and I had to throw their food on the sloping ground. Forty pairs of flat feet soon made a muddy mess of the area, stamping some of the grain into the earth, but every precious particle was later disinterred. As they ate, beaks would become filled with mud and a quick sortie had to be made to the water to rinse their tongues.

There was always much competition to eat fast before one's neighbors got all the food. The ducks scuffled and pushed. Sharp pecks were traded and wings pulled in their desperate efforts to satisfy hunger. The more timid soon retreated to the outer fringes and ate little. Even if I tried to feed the hesitant ones by throwing grain in their direction, the sudden shower upon their backs frightened them temporarily, and by the time they had courage to return the bolder ones had gobbled everything down. There was never enough to even partly fill every crop—it would have taken pounds of grain a day; I only hoped they would find additional food elsewhere.

Gradually, during the winter, some of the ducks found resting places they liked better and the numbers were reduced, but always about twenty made the Pond their home. These became known as the Mallard Breakfast Club.

I learned from watching these mallards that ducks are gentle birds; unlike coots, they are good-natured and seldom quarrel. The females scold their mates occasionally, perhaps for good reason. If one member of a duck group steps out of line, the others chase him away temporarily, but after a short swim he returns and is accepted.

I saw only one exception to this, when a duck was once judged by her fellows. It was at low tide, and very little water remained in the Pond. In a small pool five ducks and drakes were gathered, all quacking sharply at another duck. There was much conversation and what sounded like accusing quacks were made. The defendant denied it all in excited, sharp "Kuk-kuk-kuks." It was no use. Apparently a judgment was pronounced and they tried to drive her away; at first she refused to go. Sharp pecks were given and her wing feathers pulled. She twisted this way and that, trying to escape, plainly hoping they might relent. But the righteous ones persisted. Finally, she was chivied out of the pool and made to waddle off across the mud in the direction of the lagoon. I often wondered what fault she had committed which so offended the others. She had no special markings so I never knew if she eventually returned.

It was to this congenial group of wild ducks that Peter was introduced shortly after he came to live with us. He must have felt something like my astonishment at his first sight of the Pond covered with mallards. He had probably never seen any before. Standing in the corner of the land pen nearest the

water, his beak touching the wire, he studied the new arrivals eagerly. He watched intently as they gulped down the corn I threw them, and for the first time saw ducks upending themselves to search below the water. He seemed most interested in the swimming feats they performed. Eyes glued upon the scene, Peter watched their every move. To him, perhaps, it was like a show at the Aquacade. Professional swimmers, masters of the water arts, performed before his eager gaze, flashing back and forth across the surface, diving beneath it, treading water, and flapping wings. I could sense his keen excitement at this spectacle. Trying to get a closer view, he left his corner, rushed across the bridge, and stood on the deck craning his neck to see, but the walkway and its railings interfered, and he hurried back to his former vantage point. He spent hours that first day just watching, for the mallards, apparently tired from their trip, did not leave.

For two or three weeks after he came, Peter had had to be content with the pool in the pen while he watched the wild ducks' daily swim. Then, trusting that Patsy would be sufficient lure to bring him home, one morning I opened the gate and invited him to join the swimmers. Out he strode with firm and eager steps. Down the bank he waddled and plunged in.

He struck out with joyous quacks, swimming strongly with his large orange feet; back and forth he rushed. So much water! So much space! This, he seemed to realize, was his true element. He dipped his head, flung showers of drops across his back over and over again, relishing it all.

At first Peter scarcely seemed to notice the mallards, so intent was he on his swimming. But gradually he calmed down and swam happily at Patsy's side. She had already made friends among the wild ducks and, one can suppose, introduced her husband. I noticed they became part of different little groups, swimming sedately with the others. Soon they set off to explore the shore of the Pond. The tide was fully in and a breeze ruffled the sunlit water into small waves. It was a charming sight to see the ducks all bobbing up and down, and my two large white ones, accompanied by a few mallards, strongly breasting the waves as they swam across the water.

Later that day when they returned to gather near the ark, some of the drakes took vigorous baths. Now Peter could watch at close range what they did next. He had seen this only from a distance before. Intently he observed as they effortlessly rose upon their tails, trod water rapidly, flapped their wings in great arcs, folded them smartly, and sat down.

At once Peter tried to copy this maneuver. He stood on his tail, trod water, lost his balance, and fell over sideways. Poor Peter! How humiliated he must have felt! So many watching eyes and he, an adult drake, unable to execute this basic movement. The pen pool was too shallow for him to try this. I noticed he did not then try again.

But the next day, after the mallards had left for their daily jaunts, Peter began practicing. I could almost hear him giving himself directions.

"Up on the tail! Tread fast with your feet! Raise your wings and . . . oooops!" Down he would fall to the left.

"Too much pressure with the right wing. Try again. Up on the tail. Tread water. Raise both wings slowly. Flap carefully —twice is enough, don't push your luck—oh dear!" Flat on his chest this time.

At this point he would lie quietly for a moment, recovering his breath and apparently thinking through the failure of the last attempt. Then he would start again.

". . . flap carefully. Fold your wings. Now let down easily and gracefully the way the others do. There! That's more like it! Now lean forward, shake the tail, and relax. I did it!"

There were other things Peter learned from watching: how to swim underwater and how to beat his way across the surface with the aid of his wings. It was all fun. He learned to dive, to swish this way and that under water at great speed and to turn in lightninglike changes of direction. His lessons learned, he applied them by flirting about in the water, then charging among a group of ducks, his wake causing them to bob wildly about. Then he would dive and suddenly surface nearby.

When I let the ducks out of their pen, Patsy usually stayed in the Pond area. Occasionally she'd get independent and swim into the lagoon to have a look around. I would run out onto the mud spit and throw small stones near her to turn her course. This scared her and she'd scurry home.

But Peter, male-like, was far more independent. After he had acquired finesse in his swimming, he evidently longed for a larger sphere than the Pond. Let out of the pen, he'd be content for a while swimming near the ark; then when a little group of ducks would start for the lagoon, he'd join them. If I saw him, I'd toss a warning stone or two, only to see him swim out of range and pursue his merry way, quacking his determination.

This had to stop as it wasn't safe for him to go out into the Bay itself. He lacked the wild instincts of the mallards toward the dangers posed by man and beast. A couple of really persistent dogs could swim out after him, and, unlike mallards, Pekins are too heavy-bodied to fly. His few attempts took him only about three feet off the ground and four feet forward.

One day when he returned from going out too far, I scolded him and thrust him into the pen. There he stayed for several days. He stood for hours in the corner of the pen nearest the water, watching the others, plainly longing to be out.

After three or four days, I released him with a warning. "Now, Peter, don't go far or you'll be shut in again." He swam off, stayed near the ark, and came promptly when I called him. I praised this obedience, which continued for some time.

A few weeks later I heard Patsy call me. She was standing on the bank, excitedly quacking as Peter headed into the lagoon. I added my calls to hers, eventually crossing to the peninsula to throw stones at him to force him back. Patsy didn't like him to swim off either, so willingly cooperated to keep him in bounds. After some weeks he'd forget about being shut up and become independent, swimming off as he pleased. Once again the gate would be shut on him and he had to view the world from the pen with longing glances out across the water.

CHAPTER 7

Waterfront

LIVING ON THE waterfront was fun—a memory to be cherished.

In the East, years before, I'd spent many happy summer months at our New Jersey beach cottage, built close to high-tide line, a place I reveled in because of the water's proximity. Each day the ocean was different in color, movement, and sound. Here too the Bay's colors were constantly changing; sometimes the water was gray patched with silver, sometimes a varied blue, occasionally a greenish brown. At dawn or sunset it was frequently placid and touched with delicate pink; while at night it was dark as blue-black ink, with fragmented streaks of yellow orange dripping down, as it were, from lights in the hillside homes across the water.

The Bay's movements were sometimes boisterous, sometimes stilled to a moody calm. On gusty days the wind lashed up white crests on the waves and hurried them up or down the Bay, driving them along with an imperious will. If the wind was from the north, waves rushed through the lagoon toward the nearest arks, slapped against the pilings, and flowed on into the Pond with lessened force. On calm days the Pond's surface was patterned only by a solitary coot's wake, the spasmodic strides of a water-beetle, or bubbles ascending from one of the fraternity under water.

In the mornings it was a pleasure to wake up. No matter what the day, the disasters, the defeats—there was recompense outdoors. There is something so on-going about Nature, so heartening—the scene is never static. If it's dull one day, the next is likely to be sunny. If it's dry and dusty, a later heavy dew or drizzle will freshen things up. And if the day is cross or twitchety, the evening may be one of calm splendor with the benison of a golden moon riding high. At the Pond such wonderful gifts of Nature abounded.

In the early gray of dawn the first sound to be heard as I lay in bed was the distant chugging of the fishing boats. Boatload after boatload of sleepy-eyed fishermen, braced with coffee, set forth with optimistic hopes from nearby piers toward the Golden Gate and the fishing grounds beyond. Nine hours later they would return, happy, resigned, or morose, depending on what the catch might be.

Next, sleepy sparrows chirped a few notes, followed by slow wing beats as a solitary sea gull crossed overhead, bound for the ocean. Soon I could hear Patsy and Peter rise, waddle to the water bowl, slurp a few swallows, then slowly splodge-foot across the bridge to the land pen for a dip in the pool. In a short while Patsy would return to stand under the window and quack for breakfast.

By this time it was half light, the sun's coming preceded by a rosy glow. From the Pond itself came the sound of splashes as first one then another of the wild ducks plopped down onto its surface, having spent the night nearby. When most had arrived they too began to call for their food.

Now from the street came the sound of more traffic; early risers were off to work. Soon the boatyard whistle would blow. It was time to get up.

Looking out, Mount Tam usually caught my attention first. By now its summit was a misty pink while the lower slopes were still heavily shadowed. High up on a ridge a red glass eye gleamed where a window viewed the appearing sun. Across the Bay the Tiburon hills were also washed with pink, and I could see cars moving along the highway like beads on an abacus.

Then, abruptly, the nearby clamoring from the mallards and Patsy, and a splashing in the bathroom reminded me of duty. The family must be fed.

Yes, I loved being on the waterfront, for although it was close to the village there was a pleasant feeling of remoteness. One could observe human activity from afar and yet not be a part of it. The arks and Pond were an isle of privacy.

The outer edge of the bar between us and the Bay was made of sand and clamshells, with a few old timbers strewn about. Here one could sit close to the water in silence and solitude, watching sea gulls flying purposefully through the air or standing motionless on corralled logs nearby. At intervals a pelican flapped heavily by or suddenly swooped down to scoop up a fish, gulp it down, and come to rest on one of the pilings. A line of black cormorants planed deliberately across the Bay's surface toward the Golden Gate and the open ocean in a gently undulating ribbon. From time to time the leader increased momentum with slowly flapping wings, and this movement flowed along the line from beginning to end as one after another the birds joined the rhythm of his wing beat. Then, when the leader folded his wings and once again glided smoothly on the air currents, all who followed glided also.

On the bottom a few feet away from shore rested the rotting sides of an old boat. Rusty iron bolts protruded at intervals, and the whole was covered with lacy seaweed which swayed gently back and forth with the water's movement. Inquisitive small fish swam up to search the crevices for food. Once while sitting there I saw a magnificent jellyfish approach. It was about a foot across, and swam toward me with a gentle wave-like motion along its outer edge. Inside, it was hibiscus pink with spots of burgundy.

At the northern edge of the Pond garden debris and leaves were dumped, extending gradually outward into the Pond. Here a handsome black crow couple, "the General" and Maudie, often searched for grubs and insects. They spent most of the day in and about the area but slept elsewhere. They were as watchful as bluejays and would cry an alarm at any seeming danger, often aided by Patsy's loud "Aaaaaark-aaaaaaarks." Later another crow couple joined them whom I named Christopher and Gorgeous, the latter because she was always strutting about and preening herself.

The small fry—Brewer's blackbirds, sparrows, and yellow warblers—gathered their food from the bushes, grasses, and plants on the bar in front of the ark.

There was also a lone kingfisher I named Ken, whose favorite perch was a huge overturned tree-root on the bank near the duck pen from which he could view the surrounding area well. He visited almost every day, a free soul absorbed in his own affairs, but interested in the other feathered folk too.

Three grebes often swam gracefully in from the lagoon, heads high, glancing alertly about. All at once all three would dive effortlessly, snaking through the water as easily as eels. I often wondered if the watching mallards wished that they too could plunge into the depths so effortlessly, instead of with their clumsy upendings and agitated strivings.

Large blue and white herons also came as visitors, finding the fishing good in the Pond. But one came for another reason.

On one of the first warm days of spring, a large blue heron flew to the Pond, landed near the peninsula, and climbed with slow and dignified steps to the top of the hump. Here, tall in his blue jacket and gray vest, he faced the sun's warmth. After a few moments he spread his wings sideways to warm his whole body. Quietly he stood for fifteen minutes or so, then lifted his wings and flapped away.

About two months later I was surprised one afternoon on returning from work to see the blue heron standing motionless under the ark. The tide was running out, the water as high as his knee. I thought it strange that he should come so close to human habitation, and remain so still. When I herded Peter and Patsy out of their pen and across the bridge to the cage that evening, he was still there. The next morning I knew why.

Looking out at the Pond not long after dawn, I saw the heron's body slack upon the water, his long legs trailing, slowly drifting out with the tide. It was a sad sight. I wondered why he had chosen to hide under the ark in his last hours. Was it for safety? Or was he responding to some vague, aeons-old longing for brotherhood with his elder brother, man, who rightly should befriend him in his dying hours?

During the winter, many other kinds of ducks touched down at the Pond and temporarily mingled with the mallards: red-breasted mergansers, the fish eaters; pintails; lesser and greater scaups; ruddy ducks. A few shy canvasbacks who spent the winter in more secluded parts of the Bay occasionally took courage from the presence of the mallards and swam in to investigate. Sometimes a brave female stayed overnight or a day or two, but usually these visitors came only for a quick look around.

On a bright day, the Bay was exhilarating, all aglitter with sun. The wild ducks were very active on such a day, sparked with the joy of life it seemed. If there was a breeze, the white-caps danced merrily. Fishing boats, anchored in the lagoon for painting, flashed white sides as they rolled on the swell. Blue jeans, undershirts, and dishtowels flapped snappily from their lines. Often hundreds of gulls, after feeding along the beaches, or stuffing their crops with eggs laid by the huge schools of herring which entered the Bay to spawn, would return to sit on the long mud spit. Some sat patiently, others nervously took off and flew about with raucous cries, then came down, wings arched high above their heads, landing gear at the ready, unsettling their neighbors.

In the winter there were wonderful storms. Then the wind piped the tune and everything danced furiously. The fishing boats in the lagoon were all ajoggle, their masts swinging like metronomes as they reeled from port to starboard. Small yachts and cruisers anchored offshore in the Bay plunged this way and that as they tugged at their moorings. Waves rushed along before the wind and tides made no headway at all. Debris of every kind was thrown helter-skelter along the shoreline. Sea gulls were tossed about aloft, and ducks were swirled around in eddies, their orange feet paddling frantically to no avail.

Any large birds who ventured into the turbulent air found it treacherous. Suddenly sucked aloft in a strong updraft, they were whirled about and sent in a swift, slanting ground-glide threatening a crash landing. They saved themselves only by tremendous wing beating which once again launched them into the air a few feet. Soon they were exhausted and plummeted to the ground to sit hunched down tight, heads pulled in, till the gale lessened. Smaller birds didn't even attempt to fly. They remained crouched in whatever shelter they had found at the beginning of the storm: under a board, a bush, or in a clump of weeds.

Patsy and Peter loved wet weather. Gentle rainfalls were a delight to them. As the rain fell Patsy would occasionally tip her head up and open her beak a trifle to catch a few drops, savoring its freshness. She also loved the aftermath of many slurpy puddles, and the wetness underfoot on deck and in pen.

But stormy days, she found, could be a little unnerving.

One wild rainy day she was standing on the deck between our ark and the next in a rather exposed spot, her head pulled down onto her back. As the wind cavorted about, it caused her to sway this way and that before its onslaughts. The rain poured down ever faster, and she stood yet a little more upright so the water could more easily stream off her back.

As the blasts grew stronger and keeping her footing became more difficult, she evidently felt it wise to move to shelter. Taking advantage of a small lull, she started off, splashing across the planking. A sudden strong gust caught her off guard, knocking her over on the deck. Pinned down by the wind for a moment, she couldn't move. But as soon as able she cautiously got up and, head low, scurried along the wet boards and around the corner of the ark to take shelter in its lee. This experience taught her the wisdom of retreat before a superior force. I never saw her knocked down again.

On a stormy night, it was wonderful to lie snug in bed and listen to the rain as it drummed monotonously on the roof, cascaded in waterfalls onto the deck, and plop-plop-plopped through the cracks down into the water below. Furious gusts blew sheets of rain against the sides of the ark and caused it to tremble on its none too steady pilings. On such nights I was glad that Peter and Patsy were safe and cozy in their sleeping box.

If the tide was high in the Bay when gale winds screeched from the south, the constant pressure would not release it through the Golden Gate. Water poured down from the rain-sogged hillsides all around and the Pond gradually rose higher and higher until it lapped the walkway, and waves slapped the floor under the ark. Now and again a huge log was driven through the lagoon into the Pond and struck with a dull boom against the pilings, causing the whole place to shudder, reminding us how flimsy were the arks. But they had survived in the past and most likely would in the future, I thought.

Whether gray or fine, the morning following a storm revealed much debris about the Pond. Soon the water birds and sea gulls were busy exploring to see what edibles had arrived on the storm-swollen tide. Much weed had been torn loose in deeper water and drifted into the Pond; this the ducks and coots enjoyed. Weaker members of the underwater fraternity had succumbed in the turbulent tossings—small fish, crabs, mussels fastened too lightly to their rocks—all these were eagerly sought by the gulls who didn't mind their meat dead.

The swirling water was now muddy, difficult for the fishing birds. Until it quieted and cleared, the small fish they searched for would lie safely in deeper water. But as soon as the sun shone through, the tiny fish quickly swam forth into the shallows, seeking food themselves. As they darted about, their scaly sides flashing in the sunlight, the waiting egrets and herons were on the alert to make a fine meal of the hapless fish.

And as the debris-laden stormtide finally ebbed, its rich leavings were deposited along the Pond shores and muddy bottom, providing meals for rails, sandpipers, clams, crabs, and lesser creatures. Thus, through the largesse of the storm, all were fed.

CHAPTER 8

Through Pain Understanding

WE USUALLY REGARD suffering as a most unwelcome guest and yet often, as after a storm, some good follows in its wake. Peter undoubtedly could endorse this statement, for his understanding of people came only after a painful experience. For three years the love of a human being was offered him, but he would not or could not accept it. Only through suffering was he finally willing to learn.

When Peter came to join us at the ark I saw how fearful he was of people. Longing to win his confidence, I wanted to show him I wasn't like the farmer. I thought that if I could hold him on my lap a few times, stroke his feathers, and speak lovingly to him, his fears would gradually disappear.

A few days after Peter was let out of the cage and allowed the run of deck and pen, I began to make friendly overtures. First I offered him his favorite corn in my hand, holding it out at arm's length so he could snatch it easily without having to come too close. Although I approached very slowly, spoke softly, and encouraged him in every way, he consistently refused the proffered grain. He cowered in the corner and eyed every friendly gesture with terror.

I decided the persuasive approach would take forever. It might be kinder, I thought, to get Peter over his fears quickly by capturing him forcibly. Once he was used to me, I hoped he'd enjoy being petted as much as Patsy did.

After deciding on this method, I went out on the deck one morning for the first "lap-sit" session. As I approached Peter scuttered away to the farthest corner as usual and turned to face me, trembling violently. When I came near and stretched out my hand, he hissed and swelled up his feathers. "Go away and let me alone!" he plainly said.

Dear Peter! I so wanted to tell him I loved him—that he need never fear me. Slowly I spread out my arms and closed in. But Peter had no intention of being trapped so easily. With outstretched wings and a quick rush, he flashed under the barrier of my arms and pelted across the bridge to the pen.

Later, when he came back to the deck, I tried again. This time I was ready for his feints. He did his best to elude me, but I was quicker than he and caught him by the neck. Gently I pulled him toward me, got a firm, two-handed grasp about his body and over his wings, picked him up and sat down on a deck chair.

His first reaction was to freeze. "Immobility, that's the thing," instinct must have told him. He would have seen the farm ducks practice this tactic often when a hawk appeared.

Well, this is easy, I thought, no struggle, no resistance once I get him on my lap. All I have to do now is persuade him of my friendly intentions with a little sweet talk.

Caressing Peter gently, I told him how much I admired his beautiful white feathers, his big blue eyes, his strong wings, his broad orange beak and fine webbed feet. I mentioned

Patsy, what a charming little duck she was. I reminded him of the good food he now had to eat and the wonderful pool to bathe in. . . .

Dead silence. Not a muscle twitched. He might have been stuffed. He was so petrified, so overwhelmed by terror, he could sense none of the love I tried to communicate. My well-intentioned petting and talk hadn't eased him one bit. But the ordeal had been enough for that day.

I lifted him off my lap and set him on the deck. For a few moments he stayed there, not moving, unsure what to do next. Then suddenly he bolted—across the bridge, up the steps, and into the pool—to safety!

Well, that's only session number one, I thought. Not encouraging, but I'd just have to keep on trying. In time he'd surely get used to me if I persisted. And so, day after day, we went through the same routine.

Often Patsy, ever-protective after she had accepted him, would follow him into the nearest corner when I approached, or place herself between us as a shield. Then, slightly alarmed at his fear, she would duck into their sleeping box to be out of the way. Cornered, Peter would turn to face me and squat for his take-off.

Quite often I caught him in mid-air, much to his mortification. But he never gave up. For weeks he pretended he could avoid the hateful petting by swift action to outwit the terrifying human.

Once on my lap with my arm about him, Peter no longer resisted. He was always gentle and never tried to bite me. But he made it plain he wished I'd keep my hands off him. If I put my hand in front of his beak, he vigorously thrust it from him, over and over. Sometimes when he'd pushed my hand away two or three times, I'd say in a reproachful tone, "Oh,

Peter, you shouldn't do that!" Surprisingly, this sometimes seemed to touch his hard heart and he wouldn't again try to push my hand away. On other days, when feeling feisty, he'd give it another vehement shove, plainly meaning "Oh, wouldn't I though!"

If I bent toward him to kiss his soft feathered head, he leaned away as far as possible, neck snaked sideways, keeping a cautious eye upon me. He seemed horrified to view a human face at close range. When I looked at myself through his eyes I could see why. Instead of a smooth feathered contour and neat beak, a human face has all sorts of extras—hairy eyebrows above enormous eyes, a projecting nose, and an awesome tooth-filled red orifice from which emerged sounds he'd never heard before at close range. To him, a person was a giant—as tall as a thirty-foot giant would be to us—towering above him, with four long appendages, two of them tentacle-like and hooked—very menacing to a feathered creature with only a beak or a good strong wing-blow for defense!

In time Peter's fear of me diminished somewhat but he would never come to me of his own volition, not even for tomatoes which he greatly enjoyed. He was nervous whenever I was about and would hurry away. Three years went by and I was still barely tolerated.

One Friday I got ready to leave for the weekend. My son was to feed the ducks while I was gone and put them in their cage at night. As I stepped out onto the walkway and passed the front deck where the ducks were, I had a premonition that something might happen to one of them while I was gone. It was such a fleeting impression that I had time only to think, not Patsy! before it had passed. A friend was waiting and off we went; I thought no more about it. But the feeling proved prophetic.

When I came back late Sunday afternoon, my son and a neighbor hurried over to the car.

"Peter's been hurt—bitten by a dog! He's on the deck. We didn't know what to do for him. It happened about an hour ago."

I rushed up the plank to the deck, dropped my bag, and turned to see Peter lying helpless with one leg stretched out sideways, blood on it and his wing. His eyes were filled with pain. I knelt down, gently examined the wound, and found his leg had been broken at the thigh, a difficult place in a duck. My son told me that while he was in the house, a dachshund had squeezed himself through the deck fence and attacked Peter.

I phoned the vet on call for Sunday and was told he would not be back till late. There was nothing to do but wait until morning. Very carefully I picked Peter up, put him into a box with soft hay and carried him indoors. He was very thirsty but had no appetite for food. Patsy came in too, looking bewildered at what had happened to her husband. That night I kept Peter's box close to my bed so I could give him water frequently. Patsy slept near him too.

The next morning I took Peter to the vet. He took an X ray of the leg which showed that the broken thighbone had unfortunately overlapped. Fifty percent of ducks die under anaesthesia so it would not be possible to set it properly by uniting the two ends. They would have to remain overlapped.

The problem was to immobilize his leg successfully until the bones knit—a tough job with a duck and with the break in the place it was. The only thing to do was to strap Peter's lower leg and foot close up against his upper leg and side. It was secured there by passing the bandage across his back and around the joint of his other wing several times. He was really trussed when it was finished.

I took Peter home and put him into a shallow carton, placing water where he could reach out his long neck and drink. His eyes still showed pain and he lay very quietly. I brought Patsy into the house to see him but she, not understanding, chattered away and tried to get into his box, so I had to remove her.

At short intervals I offered Peter his favorite foods but he had little appetite. I picked him up every two or three hours and massaged the muscle of his good leg, for I knew it must be painfully cramped from just sitting. At times he tried to stand, not realizing his trussed leg could not support him. In two or three days the pain appeared to be less and he ate almost as well as usual.

Patsy, out on the deck, was lonely for Peter and he for her, so I let her come into the house morning and evening. Each time they saw each other a loving quacking expressed their pleasure. But I couldn't leave them together alone, for Peter, forgetful of his damaged leg, tried to struggle out of the box to join her, or Patsy would get overexcited and climb into the box with him, treading on his wounded thigh, causing a pained "Quack!"

Each day I took Peter to work with me as I didn't want to leave him alone for such a long period. He needed to be helped to stand at intervals to stretch his good leg, and to be kept quiet so he wouldn't scramble from his carton. Fortunately the office where I worked was small and the people very tolerant. I kept his box by the side of my desk, from time to time offering him water and propping him up in a corner with his chest leaning on the edge of the box so he could stand for a few moments. At lunchtime we ate together in the car.

After two weeks I took Peter back to the vet for a checkup as his bandage seemed to have slipped a little. It was late in the day and the doctor had no time. Peter had to stay overnight. The next morning when I went to fetch him, he quacked loudly the moment he saw me, joy and relief in his tones. He had not known, of course, whether he'd ever see Patsy or me again. As soon as his box was placed on the treatment table he lunged toward my arms, reached up, and nuzzled me about the neck with his beak, running it lightly back and forth, tail wagging, eyes bright with excitement, and quacking constantly. It was touching evidence of his newfound acceptance and love. I hugged him with delight, then carried him to the car where Patsy waited to give him a warm welcome.

Two weeks later we returned to have the bandage removed. Peter's shaved leg looked strange. I noticed the web of his foot was paper-thin and gray from poor circulation. Tentatively he put it down on the table. Then we saw that in healing his leg had moved and rotated outward, away from his body, so that now his foot was no longer beneath him but out to the side. Only his toes touched the ground. We also discovered the dog's bite had severed the nerves of two of his three toes; only the inner one had any strength in it, the other two were limp.

When we put Peter on the floor, he had to walk tippy-toe with his right leg and it evidently still felt weak. The vet told me to keep him quiet and confined in a small space for a while longer until his foot and leg improved. As we said good-bye, he told me Peter was the nicest, best-behaved duck patient they had ever had.

Each day I massaged the still-tender thigh. The overlapped bones had healed together well. Gradually Peter's leg became stronger and with improved circulation the web began to look normal.

It was not long before Peter could hop-walk around on his crooked leg, using his outstretched wings as crutches. Soon he was ready to go swimming. I opened the pen gate and with joyful quacks he hobbled down the bank into the water. To his delight he found his wounded leg no handicap in this element; he was able to paddle as easily and quickly as before. I watched happily as he rejoined Patsy and his mallard friends.

Throughout his long ordeal I admired Peter's courage, patience, and cheerfulness. He was a wonderful patient. During his stay in the house we came to know each other well and he finally lost all fear of me. He had learned I wanted to help him and was grateful for everything I did, showing it by gently nibbling my fingers. When I petted him, he gave me the same sort of love dabs he gave Patsy, running his beak with a light wiggling motion up my arm or sweater, mischief and affection in his eyes.

If I moved out of his sight, he would soon call inquiringly to know where I was and breathe a satisfied "Gaaar" when I reappeared. If I went away, as soon as I returned and opened the door, he'd struggle up on his good leg, leaning against the box, and call out a welcoming "Quack-quack!" wagging his tail with pleasure, to which I always responded, "Hi, Peter!" He was a dear companion and I missed him when he was well enough to return to his life outside with Patsy.

We both learned from our days together, but for Peter the day he was bitten was truly a milestone in his understanding and acceptance of human beings.

CHAPTER 9

Ducks Have Feelings

AMONG QUAKERS there is an expression "to have a concern," meaning that a person is interested in and wishes
to help a group or an individual who needs some particular
care or assistance. Patsy too has always had a "concern."

As might be expected, since it is a major concern of her own,
it has to do with food. Not for herself, but for some of her
feathered friends. Each year, from the first autumn when she
swam in the Pond and met the wild ducks until we left the
ark, she took it upon herself to see that they were fed.

Every morning soon after daylight the mallards gathered
near the ark, and the pert, sloe-eyed females would begin to
quack impatiently, announcing they were ready for breakfast.

Often I would already have been up once at earliest dawn
to feed Madame and Peter and had returned to bed. But Patsy
would wake me again, this time not with the soft, considerate
quacks she used to tell me that she and Peter were ready for
their peas and corn, but with loud, imperative calls. As the
ducks assembled on the Pond, Patsy's excitement would mount.
I could hear her flap about as she rushed from the pen, where

she could best observe the Pond, across the bridge to the deck to stand under my window. "Quack-quack!" insistently she'd call me.

If there was no immediate response from me, her voice rose with louder and louder quacks until I got out of bed, fumbled into my slippers, went into the kitchen, filled an old pan with cracked corn, went out onto the walkway and threw it into the water for the waiting throng. Then she would run to her vantage point in the pen corner to watch with satisfaction as the ducks upended themselves and slurped it down.

Another for whom Patsy was concerned was Mr. Pickwick, our pigeon friend, so named because of his impeccable manners and dignity. One evening at dusk he had flown down to the deck railing, pattered through the doorway, and flown up onto a small table, evidently ready to stay the night. The next morning when I fed him on the front deck, Patsy and Peter came over for a closer look at this new bird—a kind they'd not seen before. Thereafter he was a regular diner, and whenever he pecked vainly in an empty bowl Patsy called me to fill it.

Although food topped the list of needs in Patsy's mind, she helped out in other situations too. Whenever a dog yelped urgently or there was a bird fight, or cats mewed, or children cried, she called me to come and help. Alarm calls from blue-jays or the Pond crows also elicited her assistance, and she joined in the chorus of bird cries with her own strong "Arrrrrk-Arrrrrks." Dear tender-hearted Patsy! Another's trouble has always upset her, and she is not satisfied until I respond to her summons and try to rescue or help the distressed one.

Ducks most definitely have feelings similar to our human ones. They show their emotions in several ways: by posture, a slight turn of the head, the angle of the neck, a few raised

crest feathers, and the expression of the eyes. Singly and together, these signs indicate the intensity of their feelings. Patsy
first began to show jealousy shortly after Peter's arrival. Until
then she had had no competition. Afterward, everything, including my attention, had to be shared. Even today, although
she loves her husband devotedly, she still wants to be Number
One.

Ever since Peter accepted me, both ducks have enjoyed a
petting before being put to bed at night. Both like to sit on
my lap, to be talked to, and have their feathers stroked. This
makes the nonsitter rather unhappy. Patsy is usually first as
she seems to consider it her right. After her turn she feels more
cheerful about allowing Peter his.

Peter, too, knows the sharp stab of jealousy. While I pet
Patsy he will often swim to the farther side of the pool and
avert his head so as not to see us. His whole body posture indicates how painful it is to watch Patsy being the happy recipient
of caresses. Patiently he waits, now and then sneaking a sideways look to check on us. Although ducks can see either
forward or backward out of both eyes simultaneously, if they
really want to study something they turn their heads sideways
and give the interesting object a full-orbed attention with one
eye only. When Patsy has had enough lap-sitting and indicates
she'd like to be put down, I turn to Peter. "Okay, Peter, it's
your turn now."

He glances up eagerly and swims quickly to the pool ramp.
With a wing-assisted jump, he launches himself up it, hop-
walks to the top, and rushes down into my arms. Before he
sits, he sometimes feels a need to flap his wings, disarranged
from the pool take-off. I say, "Flap, Peter," and holding the
lower part of his body firmly, lean away to avoid being
smacked, having learned that the bony part of his wings can

give a painful whack. He stands up very straight and, measuring the distance between himself and me, gives two or three sedate flaps, being careful not to hit me. Then, wings comfortably adjusted, he sits down, ready to be cuddled.

Patsy meanwhile has wandered off, ever in search of that elusive snail or slug. But she turns now and then to keep an eye on us. This is the time when, unknown to Patsy, I often slip Peter a few peanuts, his special delicacy.

The petting is not all one-sided. Both ducks show their appreciation and affection at times by giving me little "love dabs" with their beaks as they do to each other. And Peter's eyes, always more expressive than Patsy's, show a real warmth and love.

If I have ignored the rule of "ladies first," Patsy is quick to show her displeasure. Even this usually gentle, sweet-natured little duck has a dark side. She will peck savagely at my clothing, grabbing a beakful of cloth, now here, now there, jerking it angrily, or better still, my person. I think she enjoys my cry of "Ouch, Patsy, you hurt me!" for then she attacks even harder.

When I'm off guard, she will all at once let go the cloth and suddenly bite my arm, my lip, whatever is nearest. Her hard beak-end can give a blood-drawing nip, an ugly bruise resulting. As she tussles, a foot sometimes slips from my lap. In embarrassment and anger she hauls herself up again and seeks revenge.

Often, to help her control her emotions (and prevent further sores), I put my hand loosely around her beak.

"That's a naughty beak," I say, practicing the philosophy of "deplore the sin but love the sinner." "It seems to have a will of its own. Let me take care of it for a while." She seems pleased at this, presses her beak even farther into my hand, and stands calmly while I stroke her feathers and sweet-talk her. Momentarily I'm deluded that she has forgotten the incident that provoked her annoyance. But no! In a few minutes she suddenly withdraws her beak and stabs me again.

I think Patsy actually enjoys a fight. She seems to have a very pugnacious streak and it gives her great satisfaction to contend with people or objects. Peter watches these encounters disapprovingly. It is not ladylike. He will have to reprimand her.

And this he does when I put them into their cage. Both birds waddle into the sleeping box and I can see Peter prodding Madame, quacking at her in scolding tones. She resents the criticism and is not slow to tell him so. But though she won't admit it, I feel sure she's glad Peter "bosses" her.

On other occasions too, I've seen Peter "speak" sharply to his wife. She likes to spend much time on the platform of the ramp. From here she will scold me for any one of several reasons—chiefly because she wants me to leave "her territory." At this, Peter in the pool below will reach up, seemingly embarrassed at the way she speaks to me, poke her chest feathers and quack a strong protest, plainly remonstrating with her for unseemly behavior. Life with Patsy is not all corn and peanuts!

When I take food to the pen, Patsy must be the first to receive it or she grumbles in annoyance. Perhaps her attitude results from my breach of duck etiquette that the lady should eat first. When Peter came, I noticed he always hung back and let Patsy have her fill before he stepped up to eat. I concluded this is good manners in duckdom, to assure the mother bird of sufficient food.

Peter makes one or two exceptions to this rule, however. He dearly loves tomatoes. If he sees these being gulped down rapidly by his wife, and there seems to be some question as to whether any will be left for him, he may snatch at two or three of the remaining pieces. But at other times I have seen him let her have all the tomatoes and look deeply disappointed when there was nothing left for him.

Worms are another item for which rules are disregarded. One can imagine how delicious a juicy, succulent worm is to a duck! Peter craves them as much as Madame. When worms are being dug Peter waits on the fringes of the action, letting Patsy get her feet into the hole to take up the best position for sighting and pulling out the emerging worm-ends. I have to cast clods of earth to one side and uncover a few worms for Peter, or he would have few. Patsy is most annoyed at this. If a worm is handed to Peter, she quacks a vexed complaint or pecks my feet, urging me to greater attentiveness to *her* needs.

Patsy jealously regarded even a tiny duck as an alien. When she was about seven and still showing no signs of sitting to a hatching conclusion on her eggs, I decided to test her feelings toward adoption. I tried to find a newly-hatched duckling, but with no success as it was late in the summer. Finally I found several young ducklings and brought one home on trial. He or she was about the size Patsy was when she came to me, still covered by yellow down.

I carried the little duckling in its box from the car to the duck pen and opened the box. Out scrambled the small bird. Immediately it began a plaintive peeping, insecure in the new surroundings. Both my ducks stopped their searching in the grass and stared. Peter, as he often did when surprised, stretched his neck upward for a better view. For a few moments there was a shocked silence while the ducks considered this threatened intrusion of their quiet twosome.

"Peep-peep," pleaded the little duckling as it stared in bewilderment at the two rigid strangers.

Then Patsy, unmoved by its piteous appeals, waddled over and gave the poor young thing a hard peck. Dismayed, it squawked and ran away, but soon came peeping back, longing to be accepted by this seeming mother duck. Each time it approached, it received only further cold pecks.

Even gentle Peter, when the little duckling pattered toward him, gave it a vehement prod with his beak, plainly saying, "You're not wanted here!"

I hoped the ducks might relent or show some interest after a while so I left the small duck with them. As long as he stayed out of their way he was tolerated, but the minute he approached either Patsy or Peter he was nipped or prodded. After two days of rejection I could see the experiment was a failure.

Fortunately my neighbors were moving to a new house with a garden. They had already expressed concern for and interest in the duckling so they took him with them and gave him a comfortable home. This happened five years ago, but Patsy still remembers. If I make the faintest peeping noise she will attack me, pecking angrily at my hands or clothes, seemingly filled with jealous memories.

Although jealous of the duckling, for some reason Patsy showed no such feelings toward a hen she had as guest for a few days when about a year old. Pilgrim had suddenly appeared one day in the garden of a friend living up on the Sausalito hills. My friend kept her awhile; then, having to go away, asked me to find a home for her. Thus Pilgrim came to stay with Patsy while I made inquiries as to who might like a pet hen.

Up to this time I'd always thought the comb-and-wattle set

rather stupid. The vacant stare into space while scratching, the flustered reaction to menacing objects, the proud cackles just because an egg was laid—all seemed rather inane. But I learned that I was the stupid one, that hens too are intelligent, and have a highly ordered social group with its pecking rules. After watching Patsy lay an egg, a proud cackle no longer seemed an egoistic attention-getter, but justly deserved self-praise for a job well done.

Patsy had never seen a hen before. When I put Pilgrim into the pen she stared silently, head turned sideways for the best view of this strange-looking bird-from-Mars, with the red-rimmed eyes and flaming red wattles and comb. It took her some moments to make a complete inspection.

Pilgrim felt no diffidence at all in making herself at home. She immediately began to make the rounds of the wire fencing where grass grew, exploring here and there with her beak for food. Then she tried a tentative scratching in the hard earth. Patsy watched this odd activity with astonishment; then, curiosity satisfied, she waddled across the bridge to the deck. Pilgrim followed and, discovering the food bowls, happily helped herself to a few beakfuls and drank some water.

Later, when I opened the pen gate, both birds went out eagerly onto the bar. Patsy headed for a moist, grassy area near the water where it was soft enough to probe with her beak and started looking for worms and sowbugs. Pilgrim, noting that the earth there was workable, hurried up beside her and began to scratch, at which Patsy jumped aside, fearful of the clods flying in her direction. She waddled away and tried digging in another place. Again, up rushed the visitor. Darting her head this way and that with nervous twitchy movements which set her red earring-wattles bouncing, she examined the hole Patsy was making. Patsy gave her a cold look and wandered off.

This time she waited till the visitor was busy; then she tried once more. It was no use. Pilgrim ran over to look in the hole, getting in the way of Patsy's efforts, much to her annoyance. Madame was plainly disgusted. She turned away and gave up her digging for the day. When I found a home for Pilgrim and she departed, I could almost feel Patsy's relief at having the pen and deck to herself again.

Although she shows little maternal instinct, Patsy does not lack courage, as I learned one day when I took her to visit a friend who had a delightful garden. Patsy had a happy time poking about in the borders finding tasty slugs and snails among the flowers.

My friend also had a large collie named David. After Patsy had filled her crop in the garden, we went over to the patio where David was lying in the sun, comfortably at ease. I stopped to pet him. Immediately Patsy bustled up, "Kuk-kukking" with jealousy. In an instant she hurled herself across the collie obviously trying to "drown" him as though he were a duck she disliked.

I had often noticed the way one mallard punished another either in the water or on land by a gesture I call "drowning." A duck who felt angry or aggrieved would quack indignantly at the offender and give him a few sharp pecks, then suddenly stretch out his neck and, trembling violently, hurl himself across the neck or body of the other duck, momentarily pushing it under. It seemed a useless gesture, for any duck can hold its breath and paddle a few strokes under water to get away. But it appeared to be a time-honored method of expressing annoyance. Madame has often "drowned" me!

Astonished at being attacked by this small feathered person a sixth his size, David got to his feet. Did his increased stature intimidate Madame? Not at all!

She stood on tiptoe, stretched out her neck, and with a jump and a wing flap, again tried to jump over him. David bore this nuisance with calm dignity. I had to call Patsy off and remind her of her manners, or she would have tried again.

When she was about three months old, Patsy was wandering about the living room one day. Suddenly the knitted patch-work quilt covering the bed seemed to attract her irresistibly, though it hung harmless and lifeless as always. Quivering with excitement, her head and neck outstretched, and shaking visibly, Patsy advanced toward a corner of the bed where the quilt hung loosely. With a strong beak thrust she attacked halfway up its height; then with a rush her beak traveled upward and over the top of the corner, aided by a small jump. It was over in a moment, but the encounter gave Madame intense satisfaction, for she wagged her tail vigorously. In her small mind an "enemy" had been met and overcome. The quilt survived the attack but apparently Patsy felt something sinister still lurked within its folds, for whenever she was in a pugnacious mood she would give it the "treatment." Sometimes she would catch hold of the cloth and shake it viciously before she hurled herself up and over the top.

One day to test her reactions I went to the closet and brought out a large bath towel. Shaking out its folds, I went toward Patsy, moving it from side to side like a matador. Immediately she was all attention. Body trembling, she advanced toward the "menace" and thrust hard. I shook the towel again, and again she attacked and conquered, tail wagging with delight.

It became a game for her. Sometimes when the "enemy" advanced rapidly toward her so she had to give ground for a moment, she would scold, "Kuk-kuk-kuk." Then she'd turn and charge repeatedly until finally she had had her fill of fun and walked away.

My skirt made a splendid target also. A few days after the towel game, I was standing by the telephone talking to a friend. I had on a pleated cotton skirt. All at once a hard beak struck my leg and traveled upward. Looking down I saw Patsy's head lost within the pleats. In fun, I swished the material this way and that, and she attacked again furiously —and victoriously according to her tail-wags. Evidently it was very satisfying to get the better of "mother"!

Like most birds and people, Patsy has various little foibles which add interest to life. Sometimes what I offer her in her dish is spurned with a rather contemptuous prod of her beak, meaning "No, I don't like that!" Or she will rather pettishly push the food about as though saying, "Ooooh, that's awful!" However, if I pick up a morsel and offer it from my hand she will often eat it up. Other times, if angry with me, she will deliberately scatter the food, dashing it out of the dish with her beak.

She thinks lettuce more delicious if a taste of mayonnaise or dressing is added, and a piece of lettuce from my salad, even without dressing, will be eaten with relish. Although there is plenty of plain lettuce in her water bowl, something off "mother's" plate somehow tastes better!

Knowing Madame is a bit selfish about the delicacies, I make it plain they are to be shared, putting some down by her and some by Peter. She knows quite well what I intend, but often steps over toward Peter and gobbles his portion first, then returns to her own.

It seems to be the duck's obligation, rather than the drake's, to "get the food on the table." She is the one who quacks for their meals. When she hears the slam of the refrigerator she loudly calls to remind me of their hunger. If feeding time is overdue because I've been out and they are both hungry, it is always Patsy who sets up an insistent call. Peter rarely joins in, though he is presumably just as hungry.

Occasionally Patsy would rise during the night to find a little snack. I could often hear her grumbling "Whuk-whuk-whuk," as she searched about the deck for something tasty, her beak drumming along the boards. Awakened from sleep, I'd call out, "Patsy! Stop grumbling!" Her reply would usually be a long sentence of indignant complaint, probably about the poor table I set!

From the beginning it was clear Peter too had a mind of his own, and it became even more evident after his injury. Not long after that, the ducks had a pool six feet in diameter that was entered by a long ramp leading up to a platform at the top of the fifteen-inch side and thence down into the water. When I let them out of the cage on deck in the morning, I always picked Peter up, carried him to the pen, and tossed him lightly into the pool so he wouldn't have to hop-walk the five feet up the ramp.

To get him out of the pool at night, since he wouldn't let me pick him up, I had to chivy him toward the ramp in the water; then, as he began laboriously to mount it, I'd run around to the end on the ground ready to catch him as he half stumbled, half tiptoed downward. He evidently didn't care for this slow procedure. He had a better idea—"The Flyoff!"

The next evening, when I chased him out of the water, he stood poised at the foot of the ramp a moment letting the water stream off him; then when I was about halfway round the pool, he suddenly gave a big jump and launched himself in my direction with a powerful wing thrust. Astonished, I caught him in mid-air! This was just what he wanted and he quacked his appreciation, very pleased at his cleverness. He continued this procedure for several days. Then he thought up an improvement. Why bother to get up on the ramp at all?

That night as I neared the pool and called, "Okay, Peter— time for bed," at the far side of the pool Peter gathered himself together and in a flash hurled himself dripping wet into my arms. I was flattered by his confidence—but didn't care to get soaked every night. I tried to persuade him to return to our former plan. He refused to do so. He had thought up a superior technique and intended to stick with it! What could I do but wrap myself in an old coat and be ready each night for "The Flyoff."

Soon after I had bought the ducks their new, larger pool, Patsy showed me how to play Push-Beak, a game based upon duck behavior. I had noticed that sometimes two wild ducks would meet in contest, beak to beak, each one trying to make the other give way. Back and forth they pushed, the struggle accompanied by scolding sounds, but the outcome always seemed to be quite indecisive.

But with Patsy Push-Beak was always a personal triumph!

One day when I stood near the pool she advanced toward me from the other side, paddling rapidly, neck outstretched and head lowered, her beak near the surface of the water. Her attitude was belligerent. In fun, I made a fist, and as she neared my side of the pool I met her beak with it and pushed gently. Madame was returned on her course a few inches.

"Kuk-kuk-kuk-kuk!" she said. Again she advanced, ready for the next round, tail wagging with pleasure. I pushed firmly and she was thrust backward a foot or two.

"Kuk-kuk-kuk-kuk!" That's not fair, you're stronger than I! But she returned aggressively and again I pushed her, this time almost to the other side of the pool. Bouncing about on the waves she caused, she came at me over and over until finally I tired of the game. Since she was ready to continue, she was obviously the winner and her triumphant tail wag showed it.

Peter has always been a nervous bird, nervous with people, noise, dogs (understandably enough), brooms, and, surprisingly, the harmless camera. This he "views with alarm." I can enter the pen with a book, a mug of tea, even the typewriter (for the pen being a sunny spot, I sometimes write and often lunch there, which pleases the ducks)—he sits calm and serene. But if I'm holding a camera, he gives a low warning "Qwarrrrk!" and swims to the far side of the pool. There, neck rigid, his eyes upon the menacing object, he awaits my next move. As I hold it up before my eye to get him in focus he paddles nervously about, ready for instant flight over the side if need be. I have found the only way to take a picture of Peter is to sit near him, the camera to my eye, and wait until he gets used to it.

Both ducks have very keen sight. Sometimes I'd see Patsy cock her head sideways to look up and far above would be an almost invisible airplane or a gull flying unusually high. Occasionally it was a hawk. Such a danger made no difference to Patsy; no one had ever told her about hawks. But Peter knew.

One noon when they were in the land pen, I saw Peter suddenly dive for the opening in the fencing where the bridge to the deck began. The opening was about twelve inches across and ten inches high. He quickly lined himself up *across* the opening in the same direction as the wire fencing, crouching close to the ground.

I wondered at this strange action and his very evident fear. Then I noticed a hawk circling ominously far above. Peter's keen eye had seen it too and, there being no other shelter, he very cleverly placed himself in line with the fence. If the hawk had dived, it would have become entangled before it reached him. If he'd crouched *through* the opening, either head or tail would have been vulnerable. "That was quick thinking, Peter," I told him.

Unlike Patsy, Peter has an ear for music and this became apparent his first Christmas. Playing some carols early on Christmas Eve on our new stereo, I noticed that Peter, out on the deck, was listening intently, neck stretched to its fullest extent. Thinking he'd enjoy a concert, I invited both him and Patsy into the living room where he could appreciate the full volume of sound. Patsy waddled through the door and stopped to eye the tree and decorations with much interest, but Peter moved straight toward the stereo. A few feet away he paused and, ear turned toward the speakers, stood listening with his whole being. There he stayed for more than an hour, plainly enthralled with what he heard.

After that evening, realizing Peter's love of music, I often brought the ducks into the ark to listen. I learned that Peter liked sweet, melodious numbers, especially those featuring the violin or flute, but screeching brass, pounding drums, or anything fortissimo he could not abide. To his sensitive hearing it was too much.

Music helped to while away many long hours for Peter after his injury. Because walking was a bit tedious, he tended to sit for long periods. Often I took the radio outside and tuned it to one of the better music stations for his enjoyment. He always brightened up and wagged his tail with happy anticipation when I plugged it in and the music began. As the friend who brought him to me commented once, "It takes so little to make a duck happy."

Every summer there comes a time of stress—a time of tattered nerves and tattered garments—moulting time!

The ducks' regular moult occurs in June or July. Much downy undercoating, their "thermal underwear," is shed first. This leaves them rather denuded until the new down grows in in about two weeks. After that, the larger feathers begin to drop out.

Down is actually a feather, but a multishafted one. If you examine a piece carefully, you will see there is a tiny shaft an eighth of an inch long, one end of which is attached to the skin. Sprouting from the other end are some thirty gossamer feathers about an inch long. Each feather has "barbs" (the projecting ribs) along its length, incredibly soft, and fine as milkweed floss. In down, Nature has designed a wonderfully efficient body-warmth retainer, which also keeps a duck cool in hot weather. Incidentally, a duck's body temperature is slightly higher than ours—103°.

Peter usually manages his moult rather neatly, relinquishing a few feathers at a time. Even his quills come out in only twos and threes a day, so that at no time is he really raggedy. He always looks decently dressed.

But with Patsy it's quite the opposite. Her soft feathers come out in great quantities, floating about the pen and lining the sleeping box. When it comes to quills, she often lets most of them go at one time. She may shed as many as thirty in a day, leaving the bony portions of her wings with nothing but a down and pinfeather covering. When she raises her wings to flap, from habit, there is nothing to flap! It's just a gesture.

During her moult, the few old feathers still covering her are decidedly the worse for a year's wear, and grimy too, as she doesn't bathe much while in this denuded condition. Sometimes stiff wing quills stick out at grotesque angles during this process, as they don't drop out all at once but are gradually pushed outward by the new ones and, halfway out, become askew.

Poor Patsy! She is very conscious of how tattered and slovenly she looks at moulting time. She feels all out of sorts. She appreciates much loving sympathy for her condition. Even her voice changes during the moulting and comes out as a single-noted hoarse croak instead of the varied tones she usually uses.

During these trying times I give both ducks extra-nourishing food and plenty of their favorite delicacies. Gradually, among the down and old feathers, new tightly-furled yellow ones appear. When these have unfolded, the ducks become creamy-colored in the chest, with a yellowish tinge all over for a short while. Then the color fades and they regain their pure white state once more. Each feather lies smoothly upon its fellow; quill overlaps quill, row upon row in perfect formation. The ducks look sleek, well padded, and beautiful—and they know it.

From listening to Peter and Patsy over the years, I have learned that Pekin ducks, especially the females, have quite a vocabulary of sounds. Patsy's soft "Took-took-took" connotes satisfaction. I'm greeted by this remark when I come in the morning to let them out of their cage.

"Kuk-kuk-kuk," a sharp scolding word, indicates much displeasure. If I've been slow in answering a demanding quacking, I'm told off with this!

A slow "Cluck-cluck-cluck" is sometimes a warning, sometimes a grumble. It is the latter when Madame isn't satisfied with the menu. Or it can be a sad little comment that touches one's heart, as when the cocker stole her eggs.

A low, quick "Guggle-guggle-guggle" expresses pleasure.

It is uttered at the arrival of peas or on seeing Peter after he has been out of sight.

If Patsy is unhappy over something, she grumbles "Whuk-whuk-whuk." But if really feeling sorry for herself, she makes a crying sound, high up in her beak. This is intended to soften my hard heart.

If danger threatens distantly, Patsy gives a low "Qwarrrk" like Peter. Occasionally, for no reason I can discern, she emits a loud, urgent, atavistic sound of warning, perhaps in response to a sound I cannot hear. This may continue with increasing volume for some moments. This often happened when the mallards quacked a warning; sometimes a dog's barking will call it forth. A shouted "Patsy, be quiet!" only causes her to raise her voice. She stops when she senses all is well and not before.

Peter has other words. Although Patsy seldom bothers to greet me, whenever I go near Peter he welcomes me in his pleasant drake's voice, soft and deep, "Qwarrrk-qwarrk!" Frequently when I'm in the pen he keeps up a quacking conversation or makes a comment now and again.

He indicates pleasure with a breathy "Gaar-gaaaar" if I have brought him tomatoes or peanuts, or have seated him on my lap. But he never grumbles about, as Madame does. I've never heard him give the sharp warning call, but in times of alarm he can quack loudly if necessary.

I'm sure Peter feels as deeply as Patsy but perhaps, like many men, he just doesn't vocalize his feelings as much.

CHAPTER 10

Two Bachelors and Their Brides

WHEN THE MALLARDS arrived the second autumn we were at the Pond, I particularly noticed a handsome drake among them. He appeared older than most of the others, a very alert and wise bird. One side of his beak was slightly broken, making him easy to spot. I named him Maurice.

Maurice was one of the cautious ones. When danger threatened he hung back, listening and looking, until he was sure it was safe to proceed. The following spring he mated with a plain little female, Edna, who was most attentive to him. They swam about happily with the other ducks, and were always present for the daily feeding. When the other birds left on their flight north these two stayed behind.

Soon it was May, and I noticed that Edna seldom came to be fed in the mornings. I felt sure she was nesting. Maurice also was away a good deal. He swam into the Pond area at intervals, but never stayed long. After he left in the evening Edna would swim in hurriedly, eat the food I was careful to provide, and hurriedly leave.

Then one day she failed to come. So did Maurice. I saw

him swimming about the Pond, quacking and calling, obviously searching for her. All that day he called, and the next, looking everywhere—under all the arks, at the end of the Pond, by the dump, in the lagoon, near the pier. I could see him swimming even far out in the Bay, still quacking pitifully. Some tragedy had occurred and poor Edna was no more.

Maurice had a lonely summer and I felt very sorry for him. Of the water birds only two or three coots remained plus a few visiting egrets, herons, and sea gulls. I fed Maurice every day and watched as he swam or idled on the water. When the mallards returned again in September, he greeted them joyously.

About three days after their arrival a few stragglers flew in. Later that morning I noticed a small new bird lying near the brick path by the duck pen, utterly exhausted. From the dull brown color I thought it was a young duck, though after its first moult his sheeny green head proclaimed him a drake.

I went toward him slowly to get a closer look. The poor thing in his fear tried to get up on his feet but was too weak and fell back onto the ground. I could see he was half starved, and fetched a small pan of grain and another of water, and very slowly pushed them toward him. Eagerly the little bird raised its beak to drink and eat some grain.

Maurice, who had been watching closely as he floated nearby, seemed to take in the situation. He came out of the water, waddled up the bank, and stood beside the small drake, communicating in silence as birds and animals do. Plainly he seemed to be reassuring him. "Don't be afraid, she won't hurt you. I'll stay close by and take care of you." Patsy, a few feet away, came to the corner of the pen and gazed at the new bird with interest.

All day he lay by the walk in the sun, eating at intervals and gaining a little strength. Maurice faithfully stayed beside him.

As it grew dusk, I wondered about the night. Would he be safe there with strange cats about, not to mention stray dogs? Should I try to catch him and keep him in a box till he was stronger, or was it better to leave him free?

I could see he didn't have the strength to walk to shelter—not even to the nearest bushes. But I decided that with Maurice to watch over him he would be safest right there. Even so, I went to bed a bit worried, and was relieved the next morning to see him in the same place. That day he ate more, could get up on his feet, and seemed stronger. Maurice still hovered close by, or promptly returned after a short swim. It was touching to see his concern.

I wondered where this very immature and exhausted drake had come from, and decided he must have been a very late hatch, just able to make it on the flight south with the rest of the birds. For one of his small size and strength, the long wearying flight must have pushed him to the limit of his endurance, and this, plus the fear of not keeping up with the others, must have been a terrible ordeal. Because he was such a tiny thing I called him Snippet.

By the third day I was happy to see that Snippet was much better. He was able to walk down to the bank and into the water where he swam about close to shore still befriended by Maurice. From then on, with extra feedings of fattening grain, he soon became plump and in a few weeks with his adult feathers fully grown in, he became a handsome little drake.

This was the beginning of a long friendship between Snippet and Maurice. The two were together most of the time. When spring came again and the other mallards once more left for the north, the two bachelors remained. I was glad for Maurice that this summer he had company.

Our fourth year at the ark began with a warm September. The mallards did not arrive as early as usual; generally they waited for brisk weather. I hoped very much that this time Maurice would find a new mate among them. He apparently did not fly to the lakes in San Francisco where he might have discovered a lady duck to his liking, but stayed about our end of the Bay.

Finally in October the mallards flew in en masse. Would there be a new single duck among them this time, I wondered, who would suit Maurice's fancy? Eagerly I looked them over. It was a large group but I noticed that, as usual, few ducks were unattached. And apparently none of these pleased him, or vice versa, for no romance developed. The months went by. It was January. Then one noon as I was getting lunch I glanced

out at the Pond and was delighted to see Maurice swimming
with a charming little stranger!

As keenly as though she were a prospective daughter-in-law,
I noted her attributes. She was an unusually marked little bird.
Each of her upper feathers was outlined in creamy white and
her chest was all creamy, giving her a very distinctive appearance. She stood out plainly among the other brown ducks.

I watched happily as she chattered to Maurice and the others,
dipped her beak for a drink, swam this way and that, and
finally waddled up the bank. What a funny little gait she had,
quite different from the others, as though she took smaller
steps and therefore *wiggled* along. This rear-view action probably enchanted her admirer! Even I think a duck's rear view
is intriguing. I continued to watch her that day as she mingled
with the group and noticed that she had fluttery, coy ways, too.
I named her Phyllis.

I followed the developing romance with much interest.
Maurice was a bird of experience and perhaps had had a wife
or two before poor Edna. But he was really enraptured with
Phyllis. He doted on her! His capacity for devotion had already
been shown with Snippet, but with his ladylove he outdid
himself. He followed her just as attentively as Peter had Patsy,
not wanting to be parted from her for a minute, and she seemed
to like her ever-present swain. It was a whirlwind affair and
they became a very devoted couple.

Yet the greatest devotion can be put to the test when, following the heady bliss of the honeymoon, one party continues to
demand *constant* attention. Maurice soon found this out.

Phyllis seemed to feel a little insecure in her new home in
spite of the friendliness of the other ducks. As a group they
are most agreeable to each other. There is some sharp chattering and scolding from the ladies over small disagreements, a

bit of wing-pulling if the dispute becomes heated, but on the whole they live and let live. Duck couples keep together much of the time, but sometimes one or the other will go off alone for a short swim of exploration or to look for weed.

Maurice too would swim off on his own at times and this seemingly annoyed Phyllis. If he swam around to the other side of the peninsula, the minute he was out of sight behind the hump she would start an excited "Quack! QUACK! Quack! QUACK!"

In a moment Maurice, having rushed up the farther side of the hump, would appear above its top and quickly waddle down the near slope and into the water to join his beloved, quacking softly.

At first he was plainly all solicitude on these occasions. He would swim over to her and stay close by for quite a while. But after some time, he learned that these were false alarms, really, that no danger threatened—it was just that his lady had a very nervous temperament. Who could blame him if in future he was not quite so quick to respond to her calls?

Standing on the walkway and able to look past the peninsula to the lagoon entrance to where he swam with some of the ducks, I would see him pause in his swimming at Phyllis' first appeal. With head alertly erect, he'd listen and wait to see how urgent it might be. Obviously he did so want to go out into the lagoon with the others. The cries would become more imperative and constant. "Quack, quack, QUACK!" She really had a carrying voice!

The kindly husband would finally turn aside, swim back to the peninsula, waddle up and over its hump, and patiently return to his wife, often being rewarded by a scolding "Kuk-kuk-kuk." After his years of bachelorhood and freedom, it must have been quite trying, and I admired Maurice for his unselfishness.

May is often a beautiful month. That year there were many days of sunshine with gentle breezes. The sparrows and black-birds were busy nesting for the second time, and often visited Peter and Patsy's pen to pick up a few downy soft feathers. Chattering with delight, they would hop about the pen, stuffing their beaks with several at each trip. I wondered if Patsy was pleased that her castoffs could be used by someone else. She certainly noticed the birds and heard their happy comments.

Snippet was by now nearly a year old, a fine-looking young drake with green head and bright-blue wing patches. He too went courting early in the spring and was soon joined by a sloe-eyed duck I called Sultry. They seldom left the Pond area, and often spent their time with Maurice and Phyllis. Some-times I'd go out with an extra feeding of grain and they'd all eat from my hand, with some misgivings on Phyllis' part. It took a lot of sweet talk each time to get her to try a few grains. Soft brown eyes looked at me questioningly before she got up courage to make a quick jab for the food.

One day in June, I realized Phyllis had not been about much the past day or two although I'd seen her the previous eve-ning, swimming hurriedly in from the lagoon. She had wiggled up the bank as fast as she could, eaten some grain, had a quick gulp of water, and then had rushed down into the Pond and paddled off swiftly. Maurice too was not about as usual. I wondered if she had a nest.

The next time I saw her, I watched to see where she went. Again the hurried snack, and off she paddled farther and farther into the lagoon. Then she stopped and sat perfectly still for a while, watching. Her nest must be somewhere near,

I knew, but where could she have hidden it? There were so few possible places that would be safe.

Then Phyllis, after looking about in all directions to see that no enemies were watching, swam fast toward a long cluster of dredging pipes fastened side by side, half of them floating in the water, half out, resting on the mud spit. She ducked under the nearest one and was lost to sight.

The pipes were open-ended and floated upon buoys, seven or eight inches above the water. Somehow she had managed to jump from the water into the opening and had put her nest a little way inside, well out of the reach of prying enemies. For twenty-eight days the duck mother would have to sit in that small, uncomfortable space until her eggs hatched.

Maurice was well aware of his new duties as a potential father. He spent a large part of his time out in the lagoon, apparently loitering near the pipes, but actually keenly alert to danger. In the mornings he came first to get his breakfast, then swam rapidly back to watch the nest while Phyllis came for hers. Quite often she didn't appear at all during the day, but came only in the evenings, at dusk, for a few hasty gulps of corn and a quick drink of water. Then away she swam. I wondered how she could get along on the small amount of food she ate each day. Always a fearful duck, her maternal instincts made her more so.

The days went by and I ticked them off on the calendar. Still fourteen to go. It was a long wait for both ducks. Peter would sometimes join Maurice in his quiet vigil, or Snippet would swim by to commune awhile. I was impatient for the sitting to be over.

And then, about the eighteenth day—disaster!

I had been away all morning. When I returned, I realized something was different. Maurice was swimming about the

Pond in the middle of the day. This was most unusual. Then I saw Phyllis with some other ducks. Why wasn't she on her nest?

I looked out toward the mud spit—and saw that the dredging pipes had disappeared! I knew then that a tug must have come during the morning and towed them away, as had happened the summer before.

Poor little duck! She must have been stunned and terrified to have a large snorting boat come swishing up to her hiding place, hear men's voices close by, and the clanking of chains making the pipes fast to the boat. Mother instinct must have been most urgent to stay with her nest, as she felt the pipes begin to move off through the water. I was very thankful that her fears had got the better of her and had forced her to abandon the nest for her own safety.

CHAPTER 11

The "Other Duck"

ONE WARM SUNDAY afternoon I looked out toward the duck pen to an amusing scene. There in the corner nearest the Pond stood large white Peter and Patsy side by side, beaks pressed against the wire. Exactly opposite them outside the pen stood small brown Maurice and Phyllis, just like any couple come to visit their neighbors. Maurice's beautiful green head feathers glinted in the sunshine as they all quacked back and forth enjoying a seemingly casual conversation. Only later did I discover there was more to this than innocent talk.

When Phyllis first came to the Pond, Maurice spent most of his time with her. But after a couple of years, and perhaps tiring a little of her constant demands, he began to cast a romantic eye on Patsy. They had been friends for quite a while prior to Peter's advent, and afterward both couples had swum about the Pond together many times.

Secret or unrequited longing can grow and grow even in a drake's heart, it seems. Maurice became attentive to Patsy. He often swam with her when she was alone. If she floated close to shore, eating water plants, he loitered nearby, quacking little comments.

One morning, while working in the kitchen, I looked out at the Pond. It was a gray, fog-shrouded day. Mount Tam was invisible, the water's surface glassy. The Breakfast Club were all there, unable to leave because of the fog. Patsy too sat resting on the water about ten feet from shore. Peter was across by the dump, busily exploring with his beak. All at once I saw Maurice leave the group of mallards he was with, swiftly swim toward Patsy, and, to my amazement, suddenly hurl himself upon her!

Madame squawked in horror! Churning the water with her wings, she jerked herself free and paddled fast for the bank, trying to outdistance Maurice. Hotly he pursued her and caught at her wing feathers, her neck feathers, anything he could grasp, while she twisted this way and that, trying to shake him off.

"Quack-QUACK!" she called in desperation. Help! I hurried out onto the walkway.

"Maurice, stop that! Let Patsy go!"

By this time she had reached the bank and was struggling to get up it and into the safety of the pen. Maurice, paying no attention to my command, kept a firm grip on her wing and was dragged along willy-nilly at her side. Patsy was having a hard time with his dead weight hanging onto her. There was only one way to rescue the lady.

I went down the plank, up the bank, and plucked Maurice away. Then I scolded him. "Shame on you, Maurice! Let Patsy alone!" I stroked his feathers a moment as he looked at me with his wise brown eyes, and let him go. Hurriedly he waddled down the bank and into the water.

Patsy meanwhile had rushed through the pen gate and

begun to rearrange her disheveled feathers. She stayed in the pen quite awhile before she thought it safe to return and swim with the other ducks. That day, Maurice didn't annoy her again.

Although it must have been evident to him that Patsy had eyes only for Peter and did not return his feelings, this did not deter Maurice at all. A few days later I again heard a call for help. Madame, in the middle of the Pond among the ducks, was once more being pursued. Maurice's beak clutched her neck feathers and she was vainly trying to pull away, twisting and turning to no avail.

This time, since I couldn't help her, I called on Peter to go to her aid.

"Peter! Defend your wife! Chase Maurice away!"

Peter, who had been watching Maurice's pursuit with some astonishment, undecided what to do, went into action at my words. He swam up beside Maurice, quacked a few remarks to him, and tugged hard at his wing. The latter, determined to have his way, didn't give up easily. As soon as he was plucked loose, he grabbed Patsy again while she continued to quack her distress. But Peter persisted, snatching at Maurice's feathers until he had pulled him away. Patsy, freed, paddled quickly to shore, ran up the path and into the pen. I shut the gate.

Thus began a difficult time for Patsy. She became nervous about swimming in the Pond. She had to be constantly alert and watchful to see if her admirer was at a safe distance. If he started to approach, she would quickly leave the group she was with, swim hastily to shore, and scurry into the pen calling me to come save her. Maurice often followed, and only a closed gate foiled his intention for the time being. It was very annoying for her; she could no longer feel carefree.

Her pursuer was not easily thwarted. Canny Maurice would often hide behind the large upturned tree-root near the pen or behind bushes along the water's edge, awaiting the moment when Patsy would swim innocently toward his hiding place. Then out he'd dash to give chase. There would be a flurry and a squawk as Patsy, seeing him, changed direction and sought the safety of home.

Sometimes the crafty lover would swim around the peninsula out of sight. Patsy would relax, thinking perhaps he had gone off into the lagoon. But it was another trick on Maurice's part.

From my vantage point on the walkway, I could see him swim to the farther side of the peninsula, wade ashore, and waddle up the grass-covered hump just far enough so he could peer cautiously over it. Here he paused to reconnoiter and see where his ladylove might be. Then he crouched down out of sight, only his head showing. If one of the mallards looked his way his head disappeared for a moment, then tentatively emerged again.

If Patsy was not near or was surrounded by ducks, he would wait patiently, conning the situation at intervals. Sooner or later patience would be rewarded and an opportunity arrive when Madame would be slowly paddling along near the water's edge, scouting for edible bits, happily unaware of the rapist poised above!

Maurice would suddenly emerge into full view, hustle down the slope with hot determination, and plunge into the water. Patsy's carefree meanderings abruptly ceased as she saw him. In a panic of thrashing wings, she'd let out a terrified "Quack! QUACK!" Though paddling as fast as she could for safety, Maurice often overtook her. Many times, as she gained the bank with Maurice doggedly hanging onto her wing, I had to go out and pull him off.

Often I'd urge Peter to go to Patsy's assistance but he seldom did so of his own volition. I was surprised at his nonchalant attitude. When called upon he would swim quickly toward his struggling wife and go for Maurice, pecking him here and there and finally pulling him away. Afterward he'd chase him about the Pond for a moment or two but there seemed to be no rancor over the episode. Being friends, it appeared that the tussles were mostly good-natured on Peter's part—a sort of "I say, old boy, you really shouldn't, you know. . . ." I felt Maurice sensed this or he would have desisted.

I had read that duck couples are usually faithful for life, and Maurice's conduct was therefore a surprise. None of the other drakes made passes at Patsy. All fine faithful husbands, I concluded with satisfaction—including Peter, truly a shining example of complete devotion from the very first day his eyes fell upon Patsy. And then one day my illusions were shattered.

The Breakfast Club, numbering at that time about twenty, stayed around the Pond later than usual that day. Satisfied after their morning handout, they had taken their baths, preened their feathers, and were idling on the water enjoying the warm sunshine. I had let Peter and Patsy out to join them.

By this time Peter had become quite a favorite. He seemed to be looked up to by the mallards. Being twice their size, and distinctive in color, whatever he did was easily noticed. If he swam among them, they tended to "make way" as it were— to draw aside a little to let him have plenty of room. And sometimes he would put on a show for them.

In his first weeks at the Pond, when Peter had to learn about swimming from watching the mallards, Maurice was often his model and teacher. They would swim off from the others a little, and soon Maurice would be ahead of Peter, in spite of the latter's size. I could see large white Peter putting on full steam, big orange feet flipping back and forth furiously, his body rocking from side to side a bit in his efforts to catch up with his friend. Just as he was about to reach Maurice's side, the latter would extend his wings and with swift breast strokes beat his way across the surface in great forward leaps. Once again, Peter was left behind.

The first time Maurice flapped away from him, Peter was plainly astonished. This was something new. Another challenge! There seemed no end to what a drake had to learn. But he observed what Maurice did, did likewise, and soon he too was able to streak across the water with outstretched wings propelling him forward. He loved it—the speed, the exhilaration of going fast! Quacking with delight at this newfound method of progression, and perhaps with a bit of pardonable pride at how good he was at it, he sped past Maurice, for in this size did count and his larger, stronger wings could make much greater thrusts against the water.

This day Peter was in a mood to show off. First he and Maurice swam out from the group side by side, each trying to outdistance the other. Maurice's compact little body cleaved the water swiftly, his lightness making it easy to forge ahead. Peter, not to be outdistanced, exerted himself mightily, leaving a turbulently churned wake. As he neared Maurice, the latter suddenly dove, was gone from view for several seconds, and reappeared some feet away. Peter, too, dove and apparently the joy of his watery world caused him to go suddenly wild. He flashed back and forth across the surface, wings outstretched, so fast I couldn't follow his movements, dove under a group of ducks, reappeared, swam a few strokes, then dove again and popped up in their midst, stood erect, trod water, flapped his wings, and sat down. But only for a moment. Then he was off again, streaking this way and that, his activities corrugating the placid surface of the Pond. Bobbing up and down, the other ducks followed his antics in silent admiration, even Maurice having given up the competition. Finally, having had his fun, Peter quieted down, swimming slowly and non-chalantly about.

Perhaps this show of virility went to his head. I don't know. But later that morning I was astonished to see him pursuing Phyllis! As far as I knew, he'd never given her an extra glance

before. He chivied the nervously protesting little lady through the water this way and that, herding her finally toward the bank of the peninsula. There he tried his best to mate with her. Naturally it was a fiasco; he was twice her size.

I called to him to leave Phyllis alone but he ignored me completely, so I threw some stones toward him. At that he took alarm and swam away. Phyllis stood up to flap and re-arrange her very ruffled feathers.

And Patsy? There she was, standing on the bank near the pen, watching the whole shocking scene. She looked appalled! It was unbelievable—her own faithful Peter making love to Phyllis! Rigidly erect, neck stretched tautly upward, she stared and stared, not saying a word.

What had come over Peter, I wondered. He'd never shown any special interest in Phyllis before. It couldn't be a desire to "get even" with Maurice, for I'm sure birds aren't like that. It was a mystery, one that was repeated several times that spring, and each time Patsy registered shocked disbelief, looking very unhappy.

It seems even usually faithful, attentive drakes are susceptible to the "other duck."

CHAPTER 12

Trials and Tragedy

OR ALMOST TWO years after Peter's arrival the ducks slept in the nesting box, on the deck or in the pen— wherever they liked. Ducks are not solid sleepers at night. My two would get up from time to time to stretch and flap their wings, have a little snack and a few beakfuls of water, or to wander back and forth between deck and pen and perhaps find another roosting place that seemed more desirable.

Usually Peter slept in the pool, with Patsy somewhere on the ground close by. They always stayed near each other. Sometimes they preferred sleeping on the deck under the window near my bed, and I could listen in on the bedtime conversations, soft little "Peep-peeps" to each other, just as Patsy used to talk to me. It was sweet to hear her soft, loving little voice as she spoke to her husband and his slow tender "Qwarrrks."

One lovely clear night after we'd all been asleep for some time I heard the ducks, who were sleeping under the window, jump up in alarm. I got up and looked out.

There on the railing not six feet away sat a large, handsome raccoon! Living some distance from wooded areas and across a main road, I had thought we were safe from raccoons. Perhaps this fellow had come down to do a bit of fishing and smelled the ducks. I was terrified, for raccoons are duck-killers!

Peter and Patsy instinctively recognized their deadly enemy, even though they'd never seen one before. While they stood huddled against the wall of the ark, I yelled at the raccoon to scram. He paid no attention to my shouts but sat, imperturbable.

I rushed into the kitchen to get a broom, afraid to leave him with the ducks for even a moment. Scrambling out through the casement window, I had to poke and push old "black eyes" persistently with the broom before he would leave the railing. Slowly he loped away across the deck, crossed the plank to the land, and was gone.

After that, I didn't dare let the ducks sleep unprotected. I placed Patsy's old baby cage against their sleeping box on the deck beneath the front window, and cut out part of the wire at one end to make a doorway between the two. From then on, I always put them in the cage at night, much to their annoyance, for they liked their freedom. Madame grumbled at bedtime at this curb to her wanderings, and still does.

Many pet ducks are killed not only by raccoons but by dogs. Most dogs were simply curious about my Pekins. Some of them had seen ducks only in the water where they couldn't get close enough to sniff, whereas Peter and Patsy offered an opportunity for closer inspection. A friendly dog would approach cautiously, uncertain what his reception would be and also aware he was in another creature's "territory."

Patsy, having known only the friendly neighboring boxer and some cocker spaniels, didn't regard dogs as a menace. However, if a strange snuffing nose was thrust too close, she would quack in an annoyed voice and with lowered head run toward the dog, who usually hurried away with as much dignity as possible. I always thought she showed great courage in driving away an animal so much larger than herself. Strangely, some dogs were afraid of *her*, and promptly fled when she approached, at which Madame wagged her tail with pride and satisfaction!

Almost every day I let Peter and Patsy out of their pen to wander freely about nearby or swim in the Pond, as they chose. Occasionally, an unfriendly-looking dog appeared and I'd chase him away. The ducks always remembered, and if that dog came around again, would quack in duet for me to shoo him off even though they were safely in the pen.

One morning I noticed a pair of dogs ambling about together on the bar in front of the ark—a long-haired black one and a yellow one with a coyote look about him. They were evidently buddies. Noses to the ground, they ran over the mounds of earth and along the Pond shore, finally scenting the ducks. Quickly they bounded up to the pen, barking excitedly, the yellow one especially. Obviously they would have loved to get their teeth into tender duckling. I chased them away, but they kept returning every few days. I knew they couldn't get over or through the pen fence, but even so felt uneasy.

Returning from work one afternoon and approaching the ark along the bar, I saw bunches of white feathers here and there on the ground. Alarmed, I looked up and saw with horror that the yellow dog was inside the pen. He was lunging at Patsy who, bravely standing on her nest with her back toward him, was trying to peck the black dog menacing her through the fencing. Peter was nowhere in sight!

I rushed up and hit the black dog with my purse. He yelped

and turned away. At this the yellow one also took fright and squeezed himself through the opening from the pen onto the bridge, jumped down onto the ground, and together they hurried off.

The enemy gone, I tried to discover what had happened. In the pen itself feathers were everywhere, including some bloodied tufts. I saw that poor Patsy's back from wings to tail was completely denuded and bleeding slightly.

I realized then that, although the pen itself was dogproof, the yellow dog had hoisted himself up onto the bridge, now broken from his weight, and squeezed through the small opening into the pen.

I immediately picked up Patsy to examine her. At the same moment I heard Peter's low "Qwarrrk!" from underneath the ark. I was very relieved to see him. From more feathers on the slat sides of the bridge I could see he had managed to scramble over its side and drop into the water to escape the dogs. Later I found that he too had several bare spots on his back where the dogs had tried to grab him and had taken a mouthful of feathers.

With Peter safe in the water for the moment, I carried Patsy into the ark and gently dabbed the dirt from her back. After holding her on my lap a few minutes to soothe her fears, I left her and went to fetch Peter. He came readily at my call and hurried up the bank, anxious to be picked up. His eyes had a look of terror and he shook with fright.

I took him into the ark too, and examined his wounds. Fortunately the skin on neither one had been badly broken. Apparently the dogs had got such mouthfuls of feathers they couldn't bite deeply. I decided to let the ducks sleep in the house that night so they would feel safe and protected.

It was amazing how quickly Nature repaired the damage. Down covered Patsy's bare back in three days and, in a few more, small feathers sprouted and soon grew out to full size. She seemed to feel no pain from the denuding and went about her life as usual. I repaired the broken bridge and built a strong board fence along both sides of it from the pen to the water's edge, so no dog could enter that way again.

After this episode of the dogs, life jogged on smoothly for the Pond inhabitants. It was spring again, nesting time for many of the birds. Sparrows and yellow warblers began very early to make their nests in the low bushes near the arks.

Patsy also felt the urge to start and perhaps this time raise a family. I say "perhaps," because her previous attempts had ended with impatience at the long sitting and a clutch of eggs become moribund for lack of attention. I wondered about her thoughts on starting a new nestful. Did she say to herself, "This time I really *will*!"? I don't know. Anyhow, a new nest was made, eight or ten eggs accumulated, and sitting begun.

Phyllis too started another family, in spite of the previous summer's abortive effort when her nest was towed away in the dredging pipes. I wondered where she would make one this year. There didn't seem to be any safe spot at all. But the need was imperative and a place had to be found.

About May, I noticed that once again she was away from the Pond all day, only swimming in quickly night and morning for some grain. She certainly had a nest—but where? I hoped it was not in the low floating docks temporarily moored on the shore of the lagoon for they too might be taken away at any time.

These docks were made in long sections from pieces of old

life rafts to which framing and planking were affixed on top. The raft pieces extended six inches or so inward under the planking, scarcely wide enough to support a nest and a matronly little duck, but somewhere in among the various sections Phyllis evidently found a ledge large enough. Once more Maurice took up his guard duty in the lagoon, ever on the alert for anything hostile.

A week went by. Then—again—disaster!

As I returned home one day I was alarmed to see a tug in the lagoon. A man went ashore, untied the docks and attached their free-floating end to the tug's stern.

Phyllis was on her nest, I knew, and I wondered how I could warn her. Fortunately she was frightened away by the noise and commotion. As the docks began to move, I could see her bobbing about in their wake, with Maurice circling anxiously about her. They had lost another family!

One would think this second tragedy would have discouraged Maurice and Phyllis, but Nature's urge to perpetuate one's kind is strong. The first nest that year had been an early one and within two months they had another.

This time I was completely nonplused as to its whereabouts. There was nothing afloat in the lagoon and the bare banks offered no hiding places.

One day as Phyllis swam away from the Pond I followed. I watched as she waddled across the neck of the mud spit and swam out into the Bay. She floated for a few moments, then cautiously approached a spot where several large logs were chained in a wide arc, enclosing thirty or forty floating logs tied together in twos and threes. She swam among them, in close to the bank where I couldn't see her, and disappeared.

I walked along the top of the bank but could see neither

Phyllis nor her nest among the logs or bushes. Clever little duck; she had found a place so like her in coloring, or so hidden, I couldn't find her, and I hoped neither boys nor dogs would either.

One noon several days later I was disturbed to see Maurice swimming agitatedly about the lagoon and Pond, calling, calling. I hadn't seen Phyllis that morning at the usual time and by dusk she had still not appeared. Maurice continued to call sadly.

I took a flashlight and went out to the log area but it was too dark to see anything. The next morning I looked again thoroughly—under the bank, among the logs, everywhere. There was nothing—no clue—not even a feather. Maurice was there too, searching and calling. There was no response.

Maurice was stunned by his wife's disappearance. He couldn't seem to believe it. He waddled across the mud spit and waited for hours near the site of the nest, quacking his distress. No answer. His beloved Phyllis was gone. I felt very sorry for him and understood his unwillingness to face the evidence—it was too much on top of the previous tragedies. Now he had lost two wives—and four nests!

I tried to offer comfort. When he came ashore, I fed him from my hand, then picked him up and held him on my lap, stroking his feathers.

"Poor Maurice," I sympathized. "I'm so sorry about dear Phyllis—I know how your heart is hurting."

As I said this—and I am not exaggerating—a tear rolled out of his eye and down onto my hand. Maurice well knew of whom I was speaking; all the named ducks knew their own and each other's names. I held him close a long time and he remained quiet—quieter than he ever had before, solaced a little it seemed by human love and caring.

For three days he continued to search and call. Peter plainly felt very sorry for his old friend. He watched Maurice constantly and quacked to him and, when let out, swam close to him all the time offering quiet support. It was a sad time for Maurice, but certainly the sympathetic love and friendship of Peter and Patsy helped, even as it does with people.

CHAPTER 13

Peter Gets Spanked

WHEN PETER STARTED swimming in the Pond soon after his arrival, it was Maurice who had shown him the greatest friendliness, and Peter certainly needed a friend then to show him the ropes.

He copied everything Maurice did. If Maurice dipped his head for a beakful of water, Peter did the same. If Maurice swam in a certain direction, he followed. If Maurice joined a group of drakes and ducks, so did Peter. They had always been great buddies, but there was one area of friendship where Peter drew the line. Not, surprisingly, his wife—but his home.

Sometimes, when the pen gate was open so that Peter and Patsy could go and come as they pleased, Maurice would waddle up the bank and call upon them. (This was in the days when he was a bachelor and strict monogamy was observed.) Very tentatively, at first, he entered the pen area. Then, seeing he was accepted, he made bold to waddle up the pool steps and get into the water with Peter.

At first Peter seemed happy to have him there; they swam about and talked to each other, very friendly for a while. But soon, apparently not wanting Maurice to feel too at home, Peter chased him out. Maurice soared over the fence and back to the Pond. He called several times after that and was usually allowed in for a short time to share the pool or eat a little grain, but he never felt quite free to enjoy himself.

One day when Peter and Patsy were foraging outside the pen some distance away, Maurice saw his opportunity. He walked up the bank, went into the pen, and dove into the water. Now he could glide about in the pool all by himself and drink his fill of its delicious freshness! He took full advantage of his chance, dawdling about for some time. Then he had a bath and flapped his wings vigorously.

This movement caught Peter's eye as he searched in the tufts of grass for sowbugs. Immediately he jerked upright and stretched his neck high, the better to see. For a long moment he stared toward the pen to discover who was in it. Then he recognized the intruder. Up went his crest. His annoyance was plain.

Standing his tallest and pushing out his chest, he strutted rapidly toward the pen, quacking his displeasure in rhythmic "Qwarrrrks" as he advanced.

Maurice sat tight.

Peter, rocking a bit from side to side in his hurry to oust his friend, rounded the gatepost, rushed up the pool steps, and went for Maurice.

Good-naturedly the latter evaded the attack. He tried to pretend it was just in fun. But Peter made it very plain he didn't take it in that spirit. He poked and prodded Maurice with his beak and finally hurled himself across him in the "drowning" gesture. His actions convinced Maurice he'd better leave, and he waddled out of the pen down to the Pond.

Maurice, at this time "between wives," felt free to go

wherever he pleased. Occasionally he'd join the mallards when they left for the day, or fly off to other areas of the local waterfront. (I found he called at one or two other places for a further bit of nourishment.) Quite often he swam out through the lagoon into the Bay. Several times Peter tried to go with him, but I was successful in heading Peter off.

After the other mallards had left in the spring, Maurice stayed behind. At night he usually slept on the Pond by himself. If I turned on the kitchen light late at night and he was out there, he invariably greeted me with a sleepy "Qwarrrk-qwarrrrk." But some nights he swam out into the lagoon and the gathering darkness.

Peter, standing tautly, almost on tiptoe, watched intently from the corner of the pen as his friend disappeared. Peering curiously into the mysterious unknown, he must have wondered where he went.

Perhaps life seemed a bit narrow to Peter with a world comprised only of the pen, the deck, and the Pond. He was so often frustrated in his desire to explore the possibilities of the wide world he could see from a distance, yet could not enter. This longing was undoubtedly fostered by Maurice, who would have liked Peter's company, and one night Peter succumbed to his friend's enticements.

They had been swimming together late in the afternoon in a full tide. As dusk came, I called Peter to come home. Maurice heard my call too, and must have known Peter would soon obey as he did night after night. He began swimming away while looking back. Peter sat still. Maurice circled about, swam up to him, and then away several times. His appeal was clear. Peter, wavering, followed a little way.

As I saw him apparently begin to succumb to Maurice's wiles, I called again, more imperatively.

Peter paused in his advance after Maurice, but did not turn toward home.

"Peter, come back!" I shouted again.

"Quack-quack!" called Patsy from the pen as though she too sensed his indecision.

But Peter flaunted his tail at us both and turned to accompany Maurice; they swam away together, side by side, disappearing gradually into the dusk.

For some time Patsy continued to stand by the wire fence, still peering out over the water through the gathering darkness. Now and again she called in a voice loud with concern. With tensed body and neck stretched taut, she listened for an answer. There was none. Peter had left her alone.

By eleven the tide had receded completely and I knew the drakes wouldn't return that night. Patsy was so plainly disconsolate and worried that I brought her into the ark and let her sleep in a box near my bed, as in the old days. Even after much comforting it was some time before she ceased to stand rigid, listening. At last she settled down.

I too was worried. Peter couldn't be with anyone safer than worldly-wise Maurice. But wary as he was, Maurice couldn't contend with everything; I thought of poor Edna and Phyllis. There was nothing to do, however, so we slept, though fitfully.

Before dawn, I awoke and went to the window. The far reaches of the lagoon were barely visible, the Pond outlines shrouded with mist. I gazed out into the grayness for the prodigal. Picking Patsy up, I held her in my arms so she could look out too. We watched and waited.

After some time, far off in the distance, I saw a faint movement. I strained to see more plainly. Yes . . . yes, there was a blob of white, trailed by a darker one. The erring one was returning! He was safe! Patsy could see him too but she gave no sign of recognition.

As he came closer, I could see Peter's beak opening and closing rhythmically long before he was near enough for us to hear his steady "Qwarrrk-qwarrrk, qwarrrk-qwarrrk!" I'm back, Patsy. Are you all right? The guilty inquiry of the errant male, testing the temperature of his reception.

I took Patsy outside and put her on the deck. Peter, now in home waters, paddled faster as he rounded the peninsula and came into the Pond. He waded ashore and waddled up the bank, still quacking. I opened the pen gate and in he went.

Patsy bustled across the bridge to greet him. The tone of her voice was plain.

"Kuk-kuk-kuk-kuk! Kuk-kuk-kuk-kuk!" Peter was catching it! But how relieved we both were.

Dear Peter! I felt great sympathy for his wish to see what lay beyond, for the fun of a night away from home in new surroundings, the exhilaration of the unusual. But I knew if this escapade went unpunished he'd do it again, and the taste of freedom might grow upon him. He could never take off with the other ducks since he couldn't fly, but he might swim away to other areas which were dangerous because of boys or dogs. His wanderings had to be curbed now.

So, Peter had to be spanked. He'd seen this happen to Patsy once, and was so terrified by it that afterward, whenever Madame needed a slight correction, I did it privately, out of his sight.

This time the newspaper descended upon his own wings, with "Naughty, naughty Peter!" in a very stern voice to let him know my displeasure. He flapped away, startled and squawking and, I hoped, impressed.

For several days he was not let out to swim in the Pond,

but had to watch while Patsy and the other ducks enjoyed themselves. He got the message.

When I finally let him out, I began to recall him before he'd gone fifty feet. Obediently he turned and swam back again, for which he was praised. In later swims, a few "No, Peter's" when he began to go too far conveyed what was expected of him, and he stayed in the Pond with Patsy. He never left her alone again.

CHAPTER 14

We Move Ashore

THE YEARS WE spent in the ark were full ones. Peter and Patsy enjoyed a good life there with the companionship of their bird friends and a great deal of freedom.

During Patsy's six years at the Pond, she grew from a small duckling into a mature duck. She experienced egg-laying, brief public acclaim, friendship with the water birds, and "romance" with Peter. Successfully she made the transition from a young duck dependent upon a human mother to being mate to a drake.

When she had made up her mind, she accepted Peter "for better or for worse." From her contentment it was apparent she regarded her marriage "for better." And later, after Peter's accident, when he was a little less the gay, carefree drake, the "for worse" was loyally accepted too.

I could not have asked for a finer mate for Patsy. Peter proved to be a devoted husband in spite of his occasional deviations from true fidelity. During his years at the ark he came a long way from being a "country drake" just off the farm to the gentle, well-mannered duck of his maturity.

I too found ark life pleasant, but early one spring we learned the arks were to be torn down and we were forced to move.

Sorry as I was to leave the waterfront, I realized that the decking about us was none too secure, the pilings underneath more atremble than ever, and the walkway more and more precarious every day, with loose planks tilting into the water below. The ark would not stand up forever; it was time to go.

My greatest concern in leaving was for the future of the mallards. The empty arks were to be burned. What a shock it would be, I thought, for them to fly in at evening and find the familiar landmarks had disappeared. And what would they do without breakfast in the morning?

I felt saddened at the thought of their bewilderment. For the wild ducks it meant another refuge gone. As in so many other bays and ponds around the country, humanity is greedily pre-empting the watery places, driving away the wildlife.

We were more fortunate than the mallards and soon established ourselves ashore. Life was very different and the Pond was missed by all of us, but the two ducks quickly adapted themselves to their new surroundings.

When October came the year we left the ark, I longed to go to the mountains. As usual, Sausalito had had a cool summer and I craved to feel the sun's heat for a while before the on-coming coldness of another winter. Although it was late in the year, in the mountains near the 3,000-foot level the days would still be hot; only at night would the temperature drop.

This time the ducks would have to go too for I could think of no one to take care of them. Besides, I thought they might enjoy a change.

With a rented trailer behind the station wagon, we took off one afternoon. The duck cage was in the back of the car. It was a safe place in which to keep them at night even with the windows open. It had half-inch mesh that would be proof against slim weasels which I knew inhabited some mountain areas. But Peter and Patsy rode up on the front seat beside me, each in his own box.

On previous trips I'd found that separate boxes simplified things. Otherwise Madame in her excitement would step on Peter, who was less agile after his accident, and there was a good deal of bickering. Separately, each was happy. Peter rode as most of us do, looking forward. But Patsy always turned around to look out the back. For a while they'd stand up and watch the scenery, but each traffic stop somewhat upset their equilibrium and they finally decided lying down was more comfortable.

Although Patsy had had several long car rides, she grumbled each time we set forth. I used to wonder if her reluctance was because she didn't know if we were leaving the familiar landscape of home for good. Birds and animals, like people, get attached to the familiar haunts and become annoyed at being removed from them. As we rode along I was subjected to many unkind quacking remarks and, if I leaned too close to Madame, a few good bites.

Our destination was the country near Grass Valley. Leaving at midafternoon, we had to hurry to get through Sacramento before the traffic became heavy. Even so there was time for a few quick stops to give the ducks a drink from a screw-top jar I had filled with water, and to let them out on the roadside a moment to flap cramped wings. In the valley it was still very warm, and they became thirsty often.

We entered the mountains while it grew dusk. As always, it was a thrill to begin the ascent near Auburn. While we climbed, live oak and laurel trees gave way to tall pines and firs. Among them here and there one glimpsed a splash of yellow or scarlet where leaves of oaks and maples had abandoned their summer green for a heady riot of color before winter winds seared them on their stalks and flung them to the ground. The delightful odor of sun-warmed needle-trees still lingered in the evening air. There was a freshness, a buoyancy, at this higher altitude which lifted the spirit and lightened the body.

Passing through Grass Valley, we turned off on a side road, and from it bumped down a dirt road to our stopping place on the grounds of a private school. There we pulled up beneath a small oak tree. I could barely see that we were at the crest of a downslope of fields and woods. In the distance I saw lights in the houses and dormitory where staff and students lived. The school grounds were extensive, and some cows and horses were kept as well as poultry, cared for partly by the students. I could hear snatches of conversation as the youngsters ran from the cafeteria in a large converted barn to their rooms, for in the sharp air sounds carried easily.

I got out to stretch and sniff the sweet country air, then lifted the ducks from their boxes and put them on the ground. Immediately each flapped vigorously and after a little exercise I gave them a good evening meal. Then I put them in the cage where they snuggled into the hay. Already it was quite cold and I was sure there would be heavy frost by morning.

We all slept well in the pure, crisp air. The ducks stirred only occasionally as a dog barked distantly, or at the sound of hoofs tramping past the trailer. I wondered sleepily who was on the march that night.

As the sun shone through the trailer window the next morning and woke me, I looked out to an exquisite scene. All the foreground of hillside meadow was white with thick frost, each little grass-blade and weed flower coated with tiny ice particles glinting and sparkling in the pale morning sun.

The meadow sloped away in one direction to a hidden stream whose gurgle could be heard faintly. From there the hillsides rose ever more steeply to a long wooded mountain chain gay with reds and yellows among the green needle-trees. Beyond the other side of the meadow the land fell away and away, to rise eventually in a series of mountain ranges, one beyond the other, blue-shadowed and mistily intriguing.

From the windows on the trailer's other side I could see flat and sloping fields, with trees, and a few cows browsing about. Perhaps they were the night wanderers I had heard.

Quickly I dressed and went out to release the ducks. As they stood upon the cold ground, puffs of white escaped from their beaks while they quacked to each other in surprised comment at this new landscape garbed so beautifully. Heavy frost was strange to them. Patsy tried to eat a few beakfuls, only to find it disappeared on her tongue. Disappointed that this odd substance wasn't edible, she began to inquire about breakfast and I rummaged in the car for canned peas and corn which I dished out.

The ducks' paraphernalia took up all the back of the station wagon, squeezed in beside the cage. There was a sack of hay, newspapers for the cage bottom, bags of grain and mash, their food and water bowls, canned peas and corn (they ate cooked frozen ones at home), a bag of tomatoes and another of peanuts, and in the trailer refrigerator celery and lettuce leaves keeping crisp. Quite a larder!

As the sun's warmth grew stronger and the frost disappeared, the ducks began to move about. They were free to roam as they pleased here, for in the daytime there was nothing to threaten them. The two or three dogs belonging to the school were quite used to poultry.

Soon we heard a raucous honking. Two large brown geese, who by their manner considered themselves part owners of the property, strutted up, obviously intending to assess the strangers who had appeared overnight.

Completely assured, they came up close, eyed the trailer, the ducks, and me. Seemingly we passed inspection, for after some lengthy remarks addressed to the three of us they turned about and proceeded back toward the garden where apparently they had been digging before seeing us.

During our stay these self-appointed guardians kept a close watch on all comings and goings, and any disturbance was sure to be augmented by their loud complaints. In fact, toward the end of our visit their comments had become so vociferous that the school authorities decided they must live confined some distance away, with the poultry. I longed to see more of these two characters but when I visited them in their pen, they disdained my overtures. Maybe *I* hadn't passed inspection!

By afternoon it was very warm and I knew the ducks would like to bathe and groom themselves. Down in one of the fields, not too far away, I had seen a horse trough full of water. Picking up Peter, I called Patsy to follow, and we started down the hill. Only one old horse was in the field where we were headed, and as we came near he ambled up to see what we were doing.

I put the ducks into the trough where they had a very thorough bath, ridding themselves of dust and travel-stained shirt fronts where they had slopped tomato juice.

Afterward, as I picked up Peter and we started to leave, there was a benign whinny behind us. I looked back. The kindly old horse who had been an overseer of the baths appeared so like a host at that moment that I called "Good-bye . . . and thank you!" feeling ashamed of my poor manners in having to be reminded.

Another day we went down to the meadow brook for the ducks' baths. It was a small one, three or four feet wide, deepening in one place to a small pool. It was tree-shaded and cool there, a relief from the warm noonday sun. Patsy and Peter pattered about in the shallow parts and splashed as best they could until they discovered the pool was deeper. The feel of pebbles underfoot and rushing cold water was new to them. Peter was fascinated by the bubbles made as the brook skipped over stones and playfully tried to catch them in his beak. This natural fresh-water bathing place was the first they'd experienced, and I could see they both enjoyed themselves immensely.

For some time after they had bathed we stayed by the brook. The damp ground made for easy digging, and both ducks were happy rooting about, turning up beetles and grubs.

As we walked back up the meadow, my eye was caught by something moving in the trailer. I looked more carefully and was astonished to see a white bearded face peering at me out the back window! What in the world?

Then I saw it was a small billy goat . . . standing on my bed. As I went to the door, he scampered out and away, hee-heeing. Later I learned he was the pet of one of the students and was free to roam wherever he wished. After that he came to visit us every day, and more than once got inside the trailer to stand upon the bed.

One day we took off for the higher mountains to visit a friend. Peter and Patsy went too, riding in their boxes, as I didn't like to leave them alone for the whole day.

The mountains were glorious, and I reveled in the sheer heights extending above the road and the wooded depths descending to river bottoms. We crossed several rushing rivers whose narrow canyons were strewn with huge boulders.

By noon we reached my friend's place, deep in a T-shaped chasm. At the bottom a river tumbled downhill over rocks and pebbled stretches. There on a bar formed by a right-angled turn of the river stood my friend's house and a few others. This area, now so peaceful, had once been the scene of frenzied digging for gold.

While my friend and I visited, the ducks were happy to get out and stretch their legs in the garden. By early afternoon the sun had already disappeared behind the high mountain above the road and it was time to leave.

As we traveled homeward I remembered how I had longed, when planning the trip, to see the majesty of the really high mountains. But it had been too late in the year to go to higher altitudes with the trailer. That trip would have to be for another year.

In the car we climbed slowly to the crest of a long hill and paused. Indian paintbrush and clumps of small blue flowers found a toe hold at the edge of the road where the ground dropped away sharply. To the west, beyond rows of blue ridges, the sun was already halfway down its path to the horizon. Below us, the road snaked down and down to a bridge, then twisted and turned up the next hillside.

I looked to the east. There, suddenly, through a gap in the nearby mountains I saw in the far distance a long range of snow-covered peaks. Framed in a notch of thickly wooded slopes, their pristine purity and freshness were accentuated. Serene, silent, eternally majestic, the dazzlingly white heights reached toward the brilliant blue sky. It was a soul-satisfying sight, and I sat for many moments delighting in it, absorbing it into my being. There was something enduring, powerful, pure in the scene; a memory to refresh one throughout the year.

When we reached our camp it was already dark, but a full moon soon rose to silver the landscape. I wondered about the little goat. Was he gaily dancing and tapping his heels together in some secret sylvan spot?

The next morning Peter and Patsy seemed glad to find themselves back in a familiar place. The cows and horses came wandering past us during the day as usual. The goat once again got into the trailer. Things were back to normal. In a few more days we had to leave. Everything had to be packed away again in car and trailer, and I got up early that morning to make ready.

As I put things in, some cows came up to stare in placid curiosity. Soon they were joined by two of the dogs who had often come by for scraps. Later some horses arrived, drawn by the activity of departure. When all was ready, I put the ducks into their boxes on the car seat, got in, and shut the door. At that moment, the little goat trotted up, hee-heeing a farewell. As we bumped our way across the uneven ground, we said good-bye to all our animal friends. Then, turning off the grass, we started to ascend the hilly road out.

Halfway up the hill we paused a moment near the penned geese. I beeped the horn and called a farewell. Their annoyed honking was the last good-bye to speed us on our way.

Our trip to the mountains was five years ago. . . .

Since that time, we have moved again. Peter and Patsy now have a large hillside pen, shaded by tall pines. They can still hear the distant crying of sea gulls or the barking of seals as in the old days. But their bird companions now are warblers, juncos, sparrows, and other land birds. A friendly cat often visits them too.

Peter is now ten years old and Patsy twelve. For ducks, that is "getting on"; the vet tells me nine is old age.

Dear Patsy can no longer see as clearly as she used to and her chin line droops a little. She moves a trifle stiffly at times, although when she is suddenly alarmed I am surprised at her agility. Though laid low this past year with pneumonia and a concussion, she is still vigorous. And she is still the leader, with Peter her faithful follower and admirer.

He, dear soul, is ever cheerful in spite of his handicap. Unfailingly he greets me with a joyous quack whenever I come into sight, and anything I do for him is acknowledged with an appreciative tail wag.

The pool is a continuing delight to both ducks. They are enormously pleased when it has been freshly filled, and Peter flashes back and forth across it, as he did on the Pond, while Madame bathes more sedately. Both are happy to have me as onlooker and admirer of their ablutions.

As Peter executes a fast series of bobbings, dipping his head, fluttering his wings, his tail spread fanwise, I exclaim, "Oh, Peter! Aren't you the fine, strong drake!" As though understanding my words, he redoubles his efforts and splashes even more vigorously. A like word of praise for Patsy causes her too to toss the water over herself in great showers.

One corner of the pen, always moist from filling their water bowls, breeds earthworms. These succulent morsels are carefully divided between the two ducks. "Fresh meat" is still appreciated, and in spring I collect all the snails I can find for them.

I wish I could report that Madame's temper had improved over the years. But this is not so. Jealous annoyance with me over my attention to Peter or any other live object continues. I must beware always her sharp beak, so ready to punish and put me in my place! But Patsy has her soft moments too, when she contentedly sits on my lap and seems to appreciate my love for her as I stroke her softly feathered head. We have had many happy years together, she and I.

Last Christmas I gave Peter his own radio which has given him many hours of pleasure. I like to look out to the duck pen of an afternoon to see Patsy and Peter lying cozily side by side, eyes half closed, while dreamy music fills the air. I can see that they are content.

AFTERWORD

If You Want a Pet Duck

KEEPING DUCKS *IS* fun, for all ducks have the same potential for intelligence, affection, and eagerness for life as shown by Patsy and Peter. But my advice is don't get a duck for a pet unless you are willing to accept the responsibility for housing, feeding, and loving them "until death do you part." I feel very strongly that a person who takes any animal or bird for a pet is responsible for it from then on. Of course circumstances may prevent this, but the best possible home should be found should the original owner have to give it up.

Too many people think: Wouldn't it be cute to get a baby duckling for little Jim or Mary?—little realizing the work it entails—work which a small child cannot be expected to undertake. Often the duck is either neglected or Mother has to take over. Both children and adults tire of the task and fail to care for their duck properly, or hand it on to someone else, regardless of whether that person will give it a safe and happy home.

In suburbia a duck is more work than a cat, a dog, or a caged bird. These require only food, water, and occasionally perhaps a bath. Also you have the constant company and pleasure of watching an animal or bird in the house.

But ducks must be housed outdoors. Thus, unless you can keep them close to the house, you don't see them as much, especially in cold or rainy weather when a quick trip to their pen two or three times a day is all you want to make. You can bring them into the house for an hour every day, but no longer if there is much temperature difference between indoors and outside, for they may catch cold. Keeping ducks is easier on a farm or a ranch as they can often share the hen house and pen. Some cities have laws about keeping fowl.

If you sincerely love ducks, however, and would like to have one or two about, may I suggest a few things I've learned from Patsy and Peter?

First, companionship. Like us, an animal or bird by itself often becomes lonely for its own kind, as did Patsy. Single dogs and cats are free to roam around the neighborhood to meet other dogs and cats, but ducks cannot do this. It's kinder and more fun to have at least two ducks and watch the interesting interaction between them.

Second, housing. House them comfortably and safely. By comfort, I mean a place large enough so they can roam around, perhaps twenty feet square. Just like us, ducks like to be able to wander about. Put yourself in your pet's place and ask yourself, "If I were a duck, would I be happy and content to live there year in and year out?" I've seen ducks kept in cages so low they could never stand up tall and properly flap their wings, and so small they could take only three or four steps in any direction. I wonder how the human being who keeps them would like to live permanently in a room six feet by eight feet, with never a chance to leave it. Freedom is precious to people, birds, and animals. Please see that your ducks have plenty of room.

If you have a fenced back garden, fine. The gate leading to it should have an automatic closer and a secure catch. Children, the meter reader, etc., will forget to close it, and an aggressive dog might get in and kill your pet, as happened to the pet of my friends.

So unless your back yard is fenced, make a large pen, including if possible a grass area so the ducks can root for sowbugs, slugs, and worms. If there is a wet patch too, better still.

A safe fence must be four feet high and of mesh heavy enough to withstand large dogs. The four-foot fencing that has small rectangles at the bottom increasing to large at the top, or two-by-four-inch rectangles throughout, is fine. The posts should be at least two by three inches and set about five feet apart. Be sure there are no small holes either; this is how the dachshund got to Peter. If the ground is uneven, boards fastened along the bottom of the fence will help eliminate holes.

If the pen is in an exposed, windy area, you may want to do as I have done at our present location and make a wind-break extending ten feet or so each side of the worst corner, to give shelter. I bought four-foot-wide heavy polyethylene and attached it top and bottom to long thin pieces of wood by folding the polyethylene over twice and stapling it to the strip, then nailing another strip on top. This baffle is attached with wire to the fence posts, top and bottom, on the outside.

Shade is necessary too, either from an overhanging tree or by including a small tree or bushes within the pen. If there is no such shelter, a roof on posts will serve.

Depending on where you live, whether cold at night or in winter—and *emphatically* if there are raccoons in the area—

night shelter must be provided. Remember that raccoons are duck killers and will travel a mile or more to get to ducks. They have excellent noses. Even if you haven't actually seen any raccoons around, check by asking people living some distance away if they have seen or heard any. Almost all wooded areas harbor them.

A good bedroom-nesting place can be made of a large wooden box. Peter and Patsy have one thirty inches wide, twenty-four deep and twenty-four high. This is comfortably large for the two of them. I covered the top, sides, and ends of the box with black roofing paper, folding in the ends like a package and nailing them to the box. This paper will last about two or three years, then must be replaced. I have also used black polyethylene but it is lightweight and tears rather easily. Regular roofing material is long-lasting but stiff to apply. You cannot wrap it around the ends of the box; it has to be cut to fit but, once on, it's a permanent job. I realize that large wooden boxes are scarce. If you can't find one and don't want to make one, you might be able to get a box from an appliance store that a stove or other large appliance came in. These sometimes have wood framing all around with cardboard sides. In that case, you can affix plywood or masonite to the sides.

In addition to the "bedroom box," I use Patsy's old baby cage pushed up against it at night, to make a large area. This cage is four feet long, thirty inches wide and twenty-four high. The bottom is masonite. The two sides and one end are covered with half-inch wire mesh called hardware cloth. The open end is, of course, up against the opening of the bedroom. If it's difficult to push the cage back and forth on the ground, two planks laid parallel will serve as "runners."

I also made protective covers for each side of the cage by attaching strips of wood top and bottom to a piece of polyethylene the size of the side. These were fastened on at top and bottom with pieces of wire. In cold or rainy weather they keep the cage warm and dry; in warm weather the covers can be rolled up and fastened at the top.

After I have put the ducks in for the night, I cover the top of the cage with a piece of heavy masonite, place a board along it lengthwise, and weight it down with concrete blocks at each end. If it's cold, rainy, or very windy, I partly cover the wire end of the cage with a sack, placing stones in the free bottom edge to keep it down, and weighting it down onto the roof with a brick. You can get sacks at grocery or feed stores.

Of course young ducks sleep happily outdoors in our California winters with just a bedroom box, as did Patsy and Peter before the raccoon appeared, but even in this mild climate they need more protection as they get older, very much as old people do.

Every night I cover the floor of the cage with newspaper. (Now that Peter is crippled and slips on paper, I use sacking, hosed clean in the morning.) In the "bedroom box" I put a sheet of polyethylene down first (to keep out damp—ducks can get arthritis too!), several layers of newspaper for insulation, and then hay. This bed can be changed once or twice a week.

You may wonder why bother with a cage as well as a sleeping box—why not just the latter? Well, unlike people, ducks like to get up during the night and wander about. Mine feel that even the cage and box are too small, and Madame complains nightly when I put them in. Remember that during the winter they must spend long hours there, for dusk comes about four o'clock and you can't let them out till seven or later in the morning.

I want to emphasize that the wire mesh which covers the cage must be the half-inch size. Raccoons can easily put their long skinny arms through one-inch chicken wire, catch hold of a sleepy, terrified duck, and pull it toward the wire where they can tear it apart—for what defense does a gentle duck have? And when we take on a pet I believe we are obligated to keep it unfrightened and unharmed if at all possible. Over the years I've met a number of people who told me they had had a pet duck once. When I asked what happened to it, too often the answer has been, "Oh, a dog got it"—or, "A raccoon got it."

Although certain kinds of dogs can be a protection for your ducks, the dog may not always be there. A neighbor in Sausalito kept a duck uncaged in her garden at night because her terrier slept outside. One day the dog was ill and she brought him into the house. The next morning she found her poor duck killed by a raccoon. The lesson is obvious.

Also be certain any doors or lids cannot be opened. I'm sure you've read how clever raccoons are and that their small paws can undo any kind of catch. Anything short of a lock is unsafe; heavy weights seem the best security.

It is also necessary to house your ducks well before dark because raccoons sometimes come out long before nightfall. In one house where we lived (before the ducks) a family of coons lived under the floor. In the winter they would appear at the back door for a handout as early as three-thirty if it were a gray day. If I'm going away in the early afternoon and am uncertain when I'll return, I put the ducks in the cage just in case. Better an annoyed duck than a dead one! If I'm going to be gone a day and overnight, I leave them in the kitchen, covering the floor with newspaper, so they have space to walk about.

If you are fairly permanently settled, a wire-roofed-in pen high enough for you to walk in solves this problem. But it is rather expensive and more work to build.

Hay or straw for the bedroom can be bought in bales at a feed store, or you can go haying, as I like to do, and get your own. Dry grass can be scythed, sickled, or pulled by hand. Last autumn I stuffed seventeen sackfuls, enough for a year.

Third, swimming facilities. Ducks need water to *swim* in. Of course they *can* live without a pool. We too could live without showers and baths. But it's much nicer to refresh oneself completely rather than piecemeal, isn't it? Ducks feel the same way, or more so, because they are water birds and swimmers.

Ducklings can make do with small pools, but full-grown ducks need greater depths for swimming. A twelve- or fifteen-inch pool is none too deep, as you don't fill it up to the brim. I've found that the round metal ones with a removable plastic liner are the most satisfactory. Those with fluted metal sides and plastic bottom only soon rust and are very hard to clean. Nondrain, flexible-sided pools are not satisfactory; it is very difficult to scrub the sides. They *must* have a drain; most of the five- or six-foot-diameter sizes do. Instead of using the plastic drain-closer provided, which is difficult to pull out, I found it easier to use a cork. You'll have to build a ramp up to the side of the pool, preferably with a small flat platform at the top on which the ducks can stand to preen, and continue the ramp into the pool to just below water level. You can support this end on concrete or wood blocks. I cover the ramp with sacking or old carpeting, as wet boards can be slippery. Incidentally, ducks' legs break rather easily, so keep this in mind.

The difficulty with duck pools is that in summer especially they grow algae very quickly. And of course you can't use an algae-killer since the ducks drink the water. In warm weather I may have to empty and clean the pool as often as once a week. And it's a job! The drain hole is too small to allow leaves, bits of lettuce, etc., to pass out; these stop up the hole and must be fished out.

To clean the pool you'll need rubber gloves, a large pad of medium-coarse, soapless steel wool, and an old broom. When about two-thirds of the water is out, start scrubbing the green coating off the sides of the pool as far down as you can. If it gets dry, as it does quickly, it is harder to dislodge and must be moistened first. When only a couple of inches of water remain, start sweeping the duck droppings and other debris toward the drain hole so the water will swish them down. If you let all the water out, you'll only have to run a little in to accomplish this. Then scrub the bottom, which you can do by reaching in or by stepping into the pool. Be sure you have on shoes which won't make a hole. It's most baffling to locate a small hole in the muddy bottom of a plastic liner! Incidentally, if you have to patch it, I've found contact cement is best as it bonds instantly, but it's best to wait an hour or two before refilling. You can get kits with polyethylene patches at the dime stores, or buy a small piece at a building supply firm.

If you already have a cement pool large enough, you're lucky. But this too must be emptied, and if you don't scrub it the algae will grow that much faster. There are epoxy paints you might want to use which make a smooth surface and easier scrubbing.

If you can't provide something larger, an old bathtub either sunk to ground level (drainage must be arranged) or set on the ground with an earthen ramp up to one end makes a deep pool, even if not very wide, and it's easy to clean. Plumbers often have such castoff tubs.

The fourth need is food and water. Water pans should have flat bottoms so they won't turn over easily; round ceramic dog bowls with flat bottoms are good because they are heavy. Ducks don't watch where they're going and often step into their pans, knocking them over. Be sure to leave plenty of water in the cage at night. According to Dr. D. C. Jarvis in his best seller *Folk Medicine,* apple-cider vinegar helps produce hardier, better-feathered fowls with stronger bones. I therefore add vinegar in the proportion of about two teaspoons to one quart of water placed in the cage. It's handy if you keep a bottle of vinegar near your source of water. For grain I use a heavy flat bowl too. Other things, like tomatoes, celery, etc., I put into small plastic containers. If you make a shallow tray into which two or three containers fit, they will not be knocked over.

Small ducklings start by eating chick scratch, which is a mixture of finely-ground grains, and mash. Older ducks eat hen scratch, composed of milo, wheat, and cracked corn, as well as mash. Some people serve mash dry, but it sticks to the tongue and the duck must immediately slurp some water, and the water bowl becomes soupy. I always wet up the mash to a thin oatmeal consistency. They can gulp this down easily. One thing to remember—mash quickly goes sour in hot weather or in the sun and causes convulsions, so don't leave it around for small ducklings (like Patsy) who don't know better. Ducks also like water-grass seed if you can get it at your feed store.

Ducks, like people, enjoy variety in their diet. You'll soon find out what yours like; each one has his own tastes.

These are the things I feed Patsy and Peter in addition to grain and mash:

> outside lettuce leaves (try the refuse cans behind stores for this, outside celery stalks and throwout tomatoes; the throwout lettuce and celery are darker green than what you buy, which ducks prefer)
>
> celery, cut up in small pieces; a duck can break up a stalk of celery but it is difficult
>
> carrots, cut up small
>
> tomatoes, also cut up
>
> V-8 or tomato juice diluted a little, especially when tomatoes are out of season and expensive
>
> cooked vegetables such as corn, limas, peas, green beans
>
> fruit such as melon, peaches, grapes
>
> tidbits: white or red millet, which is a little oily (from feed stores), peanuts, and other nuts

As a change from scratch feed, I sometimes buy milo alone and feed them this. Many people give ducks bread but the usual white bread has little nourishment. Peter never eats any; Patsy will occasionally accept a good whole wheat.

At one time I wondered why the ducks wouldn't eat up leftover grain until I discovered that rats had gnawed their way into the bedroom box. They have a nasty habit of "going" in the grain after eating. They also frighten ducks; Peter was bitten once in his efforts to battle one. To get rid of them, put some rat bait under the cage or box where nothing but rodents can reach it.

If your duck can get fresh meat in the form of worms, sow-bugs, etc., that is best. If not, they may like a little simmered, cut-up liver now and again. Patsy will eat only beef liver; other ducks are not so choosy. Peter won't touch it.

Another need is calcium. This is a must for all ducks both for egg-laying and strong bones. It can be supplied through dried crushed eggshells, crushed calcium lactate tablets (health-food store)—half a 10-grain tablet per duck each day—or crushed oyster shells which you can buy at a feed store. I sprinkle either eggshell or the crushed tablets on cut-up tomatoes or vegetables to be sure they get calcium, in addition to putting oyster shells in the pen.

When the ducks were loose at night, I fed them morning and evening, putting lettuce in the pool or water pan to keep it fresh. Now I put food in the cage at night; they eat their vegetables right away but there is enough grain for breakfast too. In addition I give them a noon snack, especially in summer when bedtime comes so late.

If there are few worms where you live, you may want to make a worm bed. Ducks crave them. Bits of soft fruit and vegetable leftovers stirred into the earth and kept moist will soon develop a good crop from a few starters.

The fifth necessity, should your ducks become ill, is extra care. They are very hardy and, if sick at all, mostly get either colds or pneumonia. A hot beak indicates a duck is unwell but it may be temporary and not serious. Puffed-out feathers and drooping wings mean a duck is really ill. Put it into a carton with hay and keep it in the house in a warm, quiet place, free from drafts. At night when the house is apt to chill, blankets or rugs draped over chairs, the carton in between them, help. Remember that it's colder at floor level where the carton is. If possible, keep the room the same warmth day and night. People with colds feel chilly, and birds especially feel the cold when sick and must be kept warm.

To keep the carton clean of droppings, I found it helpful to use paper towels. Peter quite understood what these were for. He called me when a fresh one was needed and would elevate his rear end a little so I could more easily take the used one away and replace it. By nature, ducks are very clean. Outdoors, if they are lying on the ground and "go," they always hitch themselves forward a little to keep their tail feathers from being soiled. Dirty feathers anywhere make them feel uncomfortable.

If your duck is really ill, take it to the vet. If it has a cold, it needs mostly rest, warmth, and perhaps vitamins which the vet can supply. Be sure there is fresh water at all times. An ill duck drinks an extra amount, sipping every few minutes. To prevent water being spilled I either use a heavy flat-bottomed bowl, or hang a cottage-cheese container in a corner of the carton. Punch two holes in the carton, one on either side of a corner about three inches above the bottom. Thread through the holes a circle of wire just large enough so the cottage-cheese container will slip into it; this keeps it upright. It makes a good food feeder also.

While sick, your duck may want only water for a day or so at first, but offer him food at intervals. Usually celery, tomatoes, and other vegetables are relished first; sometimes nuts are acceptable. When Patsy had pneumonia she liked freshly-made carrot juice with a little honey, or just honey and water; these give quick strength.

At night keep the box by your bed and check now and then

to see that there is water, or offer it if the bird is too weak to reach for itself; also offer a little food. Invalids eat little at a time so must eat more often than usual.

On my eighth birthday I was given a book, *My Pets*, one part of which impressed me deeply. Whenever one of the author's pets was ill, she sat up with it all night or rose frequently to attend to its needs. To me, a lover of bed, this devotion epitomized the worth of a pet. When childish interest flagged, I was spurred on by this remembrance. This lady recommended that an ill bird or animal be kept on a lukewarm hot water bottle to conserve its strength.

Birds and animals need to feel looked after and loved when sick and weak. I once read that the shadow of the gardener is the best fertilizer for a garden. I shouldn't wonder if the presence of a beloved owner is the best tonic for a sick duck!

A laying duck sometimes has difficulty laying an egg, a condition known as egg-bind. For some reason the egg passage lacks the necessary lubrication for the egg to pass out easily. The duck begins to stagger about strangely and strain at intervals. Fill a blunt-ended dropper with any kind of cooking oil. Then hold the bird on your lap upside down and search for the vent; it is sometimes difficult to find among the thick down. A duck cannot breathe easily on its back and will struggle to sit up, thus closing the vent more tightly, so be as quick as you can at the job. When you've located the vent, insert the dropper as far as possible and expel the oil. If some is lost outside, fill the dropper again. The egg may almost fill the opening so that you can squeeze oil only around the very entrance. Even so, it will eventually work down and around the egg, lubricating the passage.

An elderly duck who hasn't laid an egg for a long time may be unable to do so and develop egg fever. This happened to

Patsy. I had to carefully pierce the visible eggshell. The contents flowed out, decreasing the pressure, but the shell remained. It was necessary to insert my finger very gently and pull out the shell, an operation needing care in such a delicate part.

Occasionally a duck gets lice, usually around the head. If your duck scratches often, inspect the feathers and you will probably see tiny brown insects. They can be killed by a dusting of pyrethrum powder procured either from your druggist or vet. Keep your duck out of water for several hours so the powder can do its work.

I'd like to add a warning about foxtail seeds. We all know how these seeds wiggle their way through the stoutest material and they can be fatal to a bird if they penetrate the nose and reach the brain. If your duck has access to dry grass, it would be well to check each day to see that no foxtail has entered the nose. Use tweezers if necessary to take it out.

I trust you will be able to keep your ducks all their lives. If you can't and are unable to find a good home for them, some local Humane Societies will send them to farms in the country where they are given good care until they die a natural death, or perhaps you yourself can find such a place.

If in this chapter I have discouraged the fainthearted, so be it! Better to know the difficulties before you start. But I know a real lover of ducks will not be deterred. He will happily build a pen, provide safe night shelter, dig worms, supply good food, gather hay and scrub the pool—all because he truly wants "to make a duck happy!"

About the Author

CAROL E. LESTER was born in Harrow, England, but since childhood has lived in the United States. In 1940 she moved to California, always living close to the sea. Her son and his family live nearby.

To Make a Duck Happy was written to share with all who love birds the joys and happenings experienced by her two pet Pekin ducks, Patsy and Peter, and with the hope it will enlarge the understanding of those who assume birds have little intelligence or feeling. An Afterword offers advice to those who would like to keep a pet duck.

Currently Carol Lester is working on fiction for children about some of the bird characters at the Pond.